Presidents, Pilots & ENTREPRENEURS

Presidents, Pilots & ENTREPRENEURS

Lessons from the Trenches for the Everyday Entrepreneur

Derrick Jones

Copyright © 2011 Derrick S. Jones

All rights reserved. No part of this book may be used or reproduced in any manner whatsoever without the written permission of the author.

Cover design by Rita Toews

Printed in the United States of America

ISBN-13: 978-1467902830
ISBN-10: 1467902837

To my beautiful wife, Lisa, for all of her inspiration and support. I feel much stronger and capable when I am in your presence. Thank you for helping me discover the better part of myself. I love you.

TABLE OF CONTENTS

	INTRODUCTION	1
CHAPTER 1	ARE YOU IN THE RIGHT PLACE?	9
CHAPTER 2	WELCOME TO THE CLUB	15
CHAPTER 3	THE GAUNTLET	27
CHAPTER 4	THE PLAYERS LOUNGE	35
CHAPTER 5	SELL! SELL! SELL!	46
CHAPTER 6	IF I HAD A MILLION DOLLARS	57
CHAPTER 7	TRUSTING YOUR GUT	76
CHAPTER 8	TO PARTNER, OR NOT TO PARTNER	87
CHAPTER 9	JUDGE BY RESULTS, NOT BY ACTIVITY	97
CHAPTER 10	SHOW ME YOUR FRIENDS	103
CHAPTER 11	SERVING THE CUSTOMER	112
CHAPTER 12	EMBRACING FAILURE	123
CHAPTER 13	STRIKING BALANCE	130
	EPILOGUE	137
	SUGGESTED READING	151
	JOIN THE REVOLUTION	157
	ABOUT THE AUTHOR	159

Introduction

Presidents, pilots and entrepreneurs—there is something strange, fascinating and common among these three types of people. To understand one of them opens a window of understanding into all of them. They tend to have a level of confidence and bravado that far outweigh their actual abilities. This is not an insult. It is a compliment because this extreme level of confidence often enables them to overcome insurmountable odds and obstacles. From defeating enemies in wars, to breaking the sound barrier, to creating products of awe and wonder, their unwavering faith and vision gives us a far more interesting and exciting world. Making the impossible possible, the unfathomable fathomable, the unwinnable winnable. It is what makes us follow them, reject them, love them, hate them, envy them, and ultimately wish we could be them.

This book is more about entrepreneurs than presidents or pilots. While we often admire and look up to presidents and pilots, we view entrepreneurs as strange and outside the norm. That is until they hit it big. Then we call them geniuses. Nevertheless, the same admirable characteristics we see in presidents and pilots exist in larger amounts in entrepreneurs. Therefore, as fascinating and admirable as presidents and pilots are, entrepreneurs have a little something extra that places them in a class all their own.

One key difference in how we view presidents and pilots as opposed to how we view entrepreneurs is this: We see presidents and pilots after they have succeeded. Few of us witness the difficulties these men and women go through to reach their goals. Entrepreneurs on the other hand walk among us every day. They are our friends, uncles, cousins, aunts, sons, daughters and neighbors. Most of us do not understand why they do what they do and often implore them to just get a job. Then we look in awe at famous entrepreneurs on television but forget they, too, were nameless faces on crowded streets who were also told to *just get a job*. Howard Shultz, the CEO of Starbucks, was told by his father-in-law to drop his dream of building Starbucks and to just get a job. Shultz struggled at the time to get his vision of Starbucks off of the ground while providing for a pregnant wife. Fortunately for Shultz and all of us coffee lovers, his wife told him to ignore her father.

Another thing presidents, pilots and entrepreneurs have in common is loneliness. Presidents live in a bubble with only a few key people to whom they can confide. Too often they are on the lookout for their enemies and are constantly told to behave a certain way. It is for this reason that a healthy relationship with their spouse is so important. In some cases their spouse is the only person they can trust with their innermost thoughts.

Despite a huge support apparatus on the ground, pilots get lonely as they soar through the open skies. If something goes wrong up there they are on their own. However, and this is a big however, they have hours and hours of training and simulations to get them through the dangerous rough spots. Not so for the typical entrepreneur.

Entrepreneurs are lonely but for different reasons. They live in a world of possibilities; of what could and should be. Although many people have a bit of an entrepreneurial streak in them, too many fall into the category of "normal" people. Normal people often accept societal norms and primarily live in a world of what is. They allow the world around them to dictate what normal is and what it is not. Unfortunately, this results in many people going through life doing what they feel they *have* to do, not necessarily what they *want* to do.

Thank God that presidents, pilots and entrepreneurs are anything but normal. For if left to normal people we would still be riding horses instead of the horseless carriages envisioned by Henry Ford. If left to normal people, I would be writing this book by hand instead of on an iPhone or a personal computer. For one would have to be a bit abnormal to believe in the 80s that one day a computer would exist in every household. If it were left to normal people we never would have stepped foot on the moon. It took an abnormal president to make such a bold declaration.

Anyone who has ever felt that urge to go into business for themselves can certainly benefit from this book. However, it must be clearly stated for whom this is truly intended.

Those people who are members of an exclusive club of risk-takers. The guy or gal who decide to take the leap and chart their own course—the entrepreneur.

By entrepreneur I do not mean only the big names we see on television or read about in books, but also the nameless whom we pass on the street every day and whose small shops we frequent.

This gets to the heart of why I lump entrepreneurs in with presidents and pilots. Many view presidents and pilots as modern day super heroes, the mavericks of our time. Well, I see the entrepreneur as a hero among heroes. This is a bold statement and I am sure many will disagree

Most presidents are people of means. They have something to fall back on as we say. You need look no further than the list of people who lost presidential races in recent years. Most of them had enormous resources and advisers along the way. For those lucky enough to make it to the White House this is even more so.

Pilots, as gutsy as they are, get the best training and mentoring before flying professionally. They have full mastery of the machines they fly. Like fighter pilots, entrepreneurs often make split-second decisions under a great deal of stress. Unlike fighter plots, most entrepreneurs do not go through hours and hours of training simulations in preparation for tough combat. Sound decision-making is key for any entrepreneur, and many of these decisions are made purely on gut instinct. In short, entrepreneurs often have to go it alone without the massive built-in support systems of presidents and pilots.

Entrepreneurship: a Lesson in Self Worth

Most people are worth far more than the salaries they receive but only a small percentage of the population understands this. Entrepreneurs know this instinctively even if they do not express it. If every person in society truly took stock of themselves, they would realize they are worth far more than their annual salaries. Most of us have a number of natural talents, ideas and skills. We often think about our company's problems and possible solutions while brushing our teeth, eating dinner or even sleeping.

What about the PhD who creates a patented invention for his employer? A patent that goes on to earn the company billions of dollars. What do you think he or she is truly worth to their employer? Let's be generous and say their company pays them $250,000 per year? Is that enough for what they produce? Of course there is far more to pay than just salary, especially in engineering and creative fields. However, most people would not do their current jobs for half the pay, no matter how rewarding.

I remember working the graveyard shift as a security guard in my early twenties while in college, after leaving the Marine Corps. I was assigned to a large multinational company that holds a number of impressive patents. One night I was in the lobby where a number of the company's most prized patent awards were on display. Each patent bore the name of the engineer whose great mind was the source of the patent. I asked the company's head of security what the engineers received for their efforts. I do not remember the exact amount but it was not more than a few hundred dollars, and of course a great deal of recognition.

Some people place greater value on creating great works and could not care less about money or recognition. Perhaps some of the engineers on this wall were of this type, but how many people do you know who can truly say they are pleased with their jobs or their stations in life? I have met countless skilled professionals who work for large impressive companies who are not at all satisfied with their jobs. Unfortunately, many of them, as bright as they are, do not realize their true worth or value.

To be fair, no company can afford to pay every employee their true worth or value. The good news for these companies is they do not have to because most people feel they are worth no more than what they get paid anyway. For the small percentage of those who do understand their true worth, they create an environment which is in line with their vision. Some of them dedicate their lives to charitable and spiritual works with no regard for monetary rewards. Others change jobs often, not because they cannot commit or stay in one place too long, but because they desire to grow into the greater vision they have of themselves. A few others force their employers to pay a premium for their services in the form of high salaries and other perks, which the companies happily hand over. The remaining usually become entrepreneurs.

Over the years, I have often repeated a statement that I truly understood only recently. When asked by friends and family why I don't just get a good job instead of trying to run a business, I always came back with the same simple reply. No employer will pay me what I feel I am really worth. This is the psyche of the entrepreneur. There are many other people in society who feel the same way deep down inside but fail to act. You know some of them. They complain constantly about a particular job that they feel they have to keep. They feel helpless and refuse to take any sort of action that will elevate them to a higher station in life

The true value of a person lies in his or her mind and how they use it. For great entrepreneurs it does not matter the business they are in because they will likely succeed in just about any venture. This is simply due to the way they use their minds. The human mind is indeed the most prized possession on earth. A great idea that is acted upon can literally be worth billions of dollars. Every breakthrough product or service started as an idea in someone's mind. What sets entrepreneurs apart is their willingness to act on their ideas, and like great pilots, continue headlong towards the target despite the hostile fire all around.

In Hindsight

So imagine for a moment that you could go back in time ten years or so and meet up with your younger self. What would you say to yourself? What warnings would you give? What advice? Although this is not possible (some future entrepreneur will perhaps solve this problem too), one can certainly imagine. After all, imagination is the greater part of genius. Most of what you will read in the coming chapters is close to the advice that I would give my younger self if it were possible to travel back in time.

As a serial entrepreneur, I learned a number of important lessons over the years. Many of them tough lessons. My goal with this work is to share some of the more important lessons to keep you from making the same mistakes. Perhaps you just started out in your entrepreneurial venture. Maybe you struggle to stay afloat and doubt your future. Maybe you have the entrepreneurial itch and you are ready to take the leap. Maybe you have made it through the tough times and are riding the winds of success. Regardless of your stage in the journey, there are great lessons to be learned.

As an entrepreneur you need to understand that tough times are part of the great journey, not a sign that you made the wrong decision. No one makes it as an entrepreneur without experiencing extreme difficulty. There is a fine line between success and failure, and far too many people mistake the two. They run for the exit just as they approach the gates of success.

I will attempt to keep this work short and to the point because entrepreneurs are extremely busy people. Most of us will read books only about our particular craft, which are typically quite extensive. It is important however to put those books aside for now and understand your primary role. After all, you are likely already an expert in your field. This expertise alone is not what will make you a successful entrepreneur. As I often say to people, more goes into running a great restaurant than being a great cook.

You may be an accountant, doctor, engineer or retailer by trade but you are first and foremost an entrepreneur once you decide to cut the apron strings from a job. The sooner you understand and accept this, the better off you will be and the quicker you can achieve your success.

So let me commend you for choosing to become a member of this exclusive club. Sit back and enjoy the ride. The book that is. Godspeed and I look forward to seeing you in the Players Lounge.

1
ARE YOU IN THE RIGHT PLACE?

If we all did the things we are really capable of doing, we would literally astound ourselves
Thomas Edison—

Details of triumphant entrepreneurs bombard our televisions and computer screens on an almost daily basis. The public revels in the romantic tales of genius innovators amassing millions in personal earnings, but this is not the whole story. New business ventures fail at an alarming rate, leaving many to wonder why anyone would take such a risk. There is no shortage of data explaining the causes—inexperienced management, poor execution, weak business plans. To stop here misses the picture and the most basic causes of failure.

There are two primary reasons for these disappointing results, which branch off into various symptoms that we mistake for causes. For starters, too many new entrepreneurs do nothing more than create jobs for themselves. In most of these cases they would fare better by sticking with an employer. Therefore, the first requirement of a new entrepreneur is to understand and embrace this role. The skills necessary for building a successful business differ vastly from those needed for a particular profession or discipline.

Next is failure to understand the stages of the entrepreneurial process. This is akin to stepping on a football field expecting to win the game without knowing the length of the field or the incremental movements necessary to score. Notice I did not mention knowing the rules or strategy; but the lay of the field, which is far more basic. Fifty-page business and execution plans (rules and strategy) are pointless if one thinks the field is twenty-five yards instead of one hundred. What is the lay of the field? How long will this take? How do I know when I am close? Am I successful or is this temporary?

Success in business is more than starting the business, selling a product, making a profit and counting earnings. As silly as it sounds, this sums up the understanding of a large number of new business owners. There are distinct incremental phases, each with different signs and requiring specific actions. Learning to master and maneuver these stages goes a long way in reducing frustrations and unexpected setbacks. This book covers these points in detail and if thoroughly understood, will not guarantee but at least improve the likelihood of success.

The information is based on years of "in the trenches" experience, not only from myself but seasoned entrepreneurs whom I know personally. Some run struggling small companies, while others run businesses with annual revenues in the hundreds of millions of dollars. But before we delve into the details, we should first clear a few things up.

Who is an Entrepreneur?

Since you are reading this book, you either consider yourself an entrepreneur or you aspire to be one. There is lots of chatter nowadays regarding the true definition of an entrepreneur. Is an entrepreneur anyone who starts a business of any kind, even a home-based business? Should we reserve this term for those who create high growth startups that create dozens, hundreds or even thousands of jobs? There are those who insist on placing entrepreneurs of high growth startups into one camp and small businesses made of mom and pop shops in another. I am not one of them.

Webster's defines entrepreneur as *one who organizes, manages, and assumes the risks of a business or enterprise.*

The operative word in the above definition is "and." It is not enough to simply organize and manage a business. To be an entrepreneur one must also assume the risks, which brings me to my personal view of entrepreneurship.

Part-Time Entrepreneur?

Why should there be a distinction between the entrepreneur and the so-called small business mom and pop or sole proprietor types? Anyone who runs a business and assumes the risks of that business deserves the title entrepreneur. The only distinction to make is between part-time and full-time. Where is the risk for people with full-time jobs and regular paychecks with benefits?

One cannot appreciate the challenges of being an entrepreneur without facing the myriad of tough decisions and difficulties along the way. Will I be able to make payroll this month? Will I be able to pay myself this month? Can I get that order filled on time? Challenges are important ingredients in the growth and maturity of the entrepreneur. A business on the side, which merely supplements income and protects one from the true hardships of entrepreneurship, stunts this growth. Holding on to a "secure" job while calling oneself an entrepreneur is similar to a college student bragging of being "on my own" while living off of mom's credit cards and bringing home laundry during the holidays.

Some of those with part-time businesses may misunderstand and take offense to these words. There is nothing wrong with having supplemental income or planning a move to full-time entrepreneurship, but it must be stated clearly that you will not grow a sustainable business on a part-time basis. You might sell product, generate buzz, and get a nice part-time income, but you will not grow a business. If growing a business is your ultimate goal, then let this be your first lesson. Sit down and create a plan to take your business or your idea full-time. As long as you have a safety net, you will not take the risks necessary to realize your full potential as an entrepreneur. This sounds a bit counterintuitive, for if one has a safety net, would not they be more apt to taking more risks? The answer is an unequivocal no because by holding on to the safety net your mind is trained to avoid risks. The role of part-time or "on the side" is to test an idea or to get your feet wet. In fact, this is a great way to start, but substantial growth will only occur with full-time dedication.

Taking the Small Out of Small Business

Up to this point, I have used the terms entrepreneur and small business interchangeably only because people have been conditioned to separate them. This is the last time in this entire book I will use the term small business because I am not particularly fond of the term.

Entrepreneur is a big word and brings to mind names like Steve Jobs, Bill Gates, Warren Buffett, Howard Shultz and Damon John. Without any sort of effort, terms like IPOs, venture capital, product launches and notoriety flood our minds. Now what comes to mind when you think of small business?

The biggest word in small business is the word "small." We think of plumbers, corner stores or lone consultants. The people we like to tell to *just get a job*. Despite all the praise from politicians and the public at large, too often we see small businesses as just small; literally and figuratively. Not as prestigious or important as "The Entrepreneurs." This train of thought is wrong and not in this work. Anyone who *assumes the risks of a business or enterprise* is an entrepreneur. Period.

The choice is yours as to whether you are in the right place or if perhaps you made a wrong turn. Now that we have that out of the way, let us get back to the business of entrepreneurship and how best to use this book.

Conventions In This Book

Each of the following chapters concludes with the same section headings in order for you, the reader, to get more out of each chapter. The "In Hindsight" section summarizes my own experiences relevant to the lesson in the chapter. I detail where I went wrong and how you can do better. The "Key Take Aways" section is a bulleted list of the most important points of the chapter.

Together, these two sections serve as a quick reference, making it easy for you to quickly re-familiarize yourself with the lessons in the chapter.

Refer back to these sections often as you make your way through the various phases of the journey.

The amount of information available on starting and running a business is overwhelming, creating information overload for new entrepreneurs. From websites to blogs to hundreds of books, where does one start? Well, start here.

At the end of the book is a list of several books on the subject of entrepreneurship, leadership and business. This work references some of this material throughout. My list is by no means exhaustive. Nonetheless, it is a good start and will keep you from combing through mountains of material. Most of the books referenced are bestsellers and have been extremely helpful to many others beside myself. So, consider this your entrepreneurial primer. If only I had had such a work to start me off in my early days. If you are ready to pay the price let's get started, but are you ready to pay the price?

2
WELCOME TO THE CLUB

Before success comes in any man's life, he's sure to meet with much temporary defeat and perhaps some failures. When defeat overtakes a man, the easiest and the most logical thing to do is to quit. That's exactly what the majority of men do.
Napoleon Hill—

How do you know when you are succeeding and when it is time to throw in the towel? Are you deceiving yourself and prolonging inevitable failure? When is it time to hire the first employee or bring on the operations manager? Before getting into these subjects or those dealing with choosing a partner, dealing with banks or engaging with customers, we must first understand the landscape of entrepreneurship–the phases of development. For the rest of this does not matter without first understanding this important prerequisite. So, let us put those other topics aside for now while we tour what I call The Entrepreneur Club.

EXCLUSIVE CLUB MEMBERSHIP

So, what is this club thing I keep referencing? This may seem like a strange idea to some but I consider entrepreneurship an exclusive club. Think of the resorts and dining clubs that charge thousands of dollars for membership. Some are even by invitation only, granting access only to the cream of society. This club of entrepreneurship is exclusive as well but with one striking difference—prospective members enter without scrutiny or hefty fees. Membership is available to all daring enough to enter. The price of admission is not what you pay to get in, but what you pay to *stay* in.

Entrepreneurship is a great game with tremendous rewards for those who play well. Playing poorly or haphazardly, however, leads to devastating and sometimes long-lasting difficulties. As you make your way through this club, traversing the various stages, the ultimate destination is The Players Lounge. Do not be deceived by the name, as The Players Lounge is where the real work starts and the greatest risks await.

Although the club idea is a bit tongue in cheek, the phases of entrepreneurship are real. Jumping into entrepreneurship without understanding this landscape is like parachuting into an unknown forest without a map or GPS. So, what are those phases? How do we recognize them, and how do we navigate them?

THE ENTRANCE

Oh, The Entrance, where every wannabe Richard Branson flocks with visions of billion dollar IPOs and delusions of grandeur. People of all types crowd around —young and old; men and women; white, black and everything in between. As you enter, it seems odd such an exclusive club allows anyone to walk right in. You wonder if wild tales of success are too good to be true.

The price at this phase is minuscule. A visit to the local department of state with $75 to $150 is enough to incorporate and officially start a business. This takes no ingenuity or considerable intellect. Granted, this is a commendable first step toward the realization of a dream, something others only talk about. It does not, however, make you a genius of industry and is not a time for celebration.

Near the club entrance is another door surrounded by a different kind of crowd. People stumble out exhausted, beaten, and some even bloodied. *What happened to them?* Still another crowd gathers around you whose only interest is discouraging and berating those headed for the entrance. The entire scene is intimidating and somewhat confusing, but you make your way through the doors ignoring the surrounding chaos.

THE LOBBY

Like all entrants, you love The Lobby because you are the center of attention. Everyone greets you with high fives and pats on the back; much friendlier than the crowd of naysayers and critics on the outside. This is the point you start operating your business and generate some initial buzz. People show interest and sales come in, temporarily silencing the naysayers. Hence, this is where most new entrepreneurs make their first mistake. They allow the early success common in all new ventures to delude themselves into thinking the process will be easy. In actuality, success at this stage requires very little effort. Early adopters, well-wishers and enthusiasts account for much of the business at this stage. These types buy despite any shortcomings in the founders or the products. Buyers include customers poached from previous employers, supportive friends and family, and former colleagues.

Take for example, the poached client of a previous employer. What exactly did the entrepreneur sell? What deal did they broker? Someone else did the selling for them—the experienced sales team of the previous employer. This well of easy wins will soon dry up, which is why too much reliance on this type of customer is a poor strategy.

This was my experience back in 2000. The consulting company I worked for began layoffs following the dot com bust. I remember being present when some of the engineers and technicians were let go. They dropped like flies while my own projects suffered from lack of back office support. More concerning for me was the fact that I moved my wife and three kids from California a year earlier. Never one to be acted upon, I decided to incorporate a business in case I, too, was downsized. Confident I could leverage the reputation I had built for myself, I went to work planning the consulting business I always wanted. For some reason, and I still am not sure why, seeking out another job was never a consideration.

I bought a small book on the basic mechanics of starting a business and meticulously followed all the instructions; separating business and personal accounts; researching corporation types; establishing bylaws; planning sales and marketing, etc. I even had a graphics designer create a logo and business cards. I headed to the New York State Department of State, paid the fee and filed the paperwork. I was technically in business, and it all seemed so easy.

As my project wound down, I approached my employer and told them of additional opportunities with the client. All I needed was a salesperson to close the deal, but these guys were in complete disarray and fearful of losing their own jobs. I contemplated long and hard on my next move. I could close the deal for my employer with the risk of being laid off a few months later, or be more creative. I chose the latter by preparing a sales pitch and rehearsing my delivery for days.

One day while I worked on final edits to technical documentation, the finance manager of the Information Services department walked in. This was as good an opportunity as any, so I went for it. The following is the gist of the conversation.

"So, I understand company X charges X amount of dollars for my services. It seems to me this project is not quite complete and an extension is in order. You can either continue with me through company X or contract me directly for about thirty percent less. So, which way would you like to go?"

The finance manager smiled and simply replied, "I'd like to go with you directly."

"Great," I said. "What do you need from me?"

In the span of about sixty seconds, I "negotiated" my first client contract. I went on to have similar conversations with other customers and subcontracted my services to other companies where former colleagues went to work. I rode this wave through most of 2001, which started as a profitable year. I even did something I always dreamed of—walked on a car lot and paid cash for the vehicle of my choice. My income was the result of relationships with prior clients, colleagues and vendors familiar with my work. This was August 2001 and I was in the middle of another big project. By definition, I was still in The Lobby.

Rooted in the previous narrative is a crucial lesson. I did not sell anything, and that first deal I "negotiated" was not a negotiation at all. A professional salesperson won over the customer several months prior. Although I did my part by performing well and impressing the customer, someone else did the hard work of prospecting, negotiating and winning the business. The deceptive and dangerous aspect of this stage is the relative ease of acquiring customers. Although this is a fantastic way to start, it is unsustainable in the longer term because, as I stated earlier, this well will dry up.

This is not to put down or belittle my efforts, for I sensed an opportunity where most others saw a problem. Although taking the first step is commendable, it is only the first step. The mistake of many beginning entrepreneurs is they stop here to celebrate, and sometimes the party goes on a little too long. If only they knew what lies ahead, they would not stop to hear the cheers. They would continue in a full sprint.

Another example of this type of easy sell is supportive friends and family who have a tendency to overlook deficiencies. This group requires no convincing, and often purchase despite lack of interest. Think of the friend who invites you to a "meeting" at someone's home. By the end of the evening, they become a "distributor" (just a fancy way of saying salesperson) for a multilevel marketing organization selling vitamins, insurance or any host of other products. They feel a rush of excitement because of the potential of the opportunity. For the first time in their lives, they realize their dream of working for themselves, and fantasize about the television shows and magazine articles profiling their entrepreneurial genius. They entertain visions of reshaping an industry and amassing millions in the process—all on a part-time basis. Soon they rack up sales from friends and family and are stunned by their instant success. Then something unanticipated happens. They run out of family and friends, the early adopter well-wishers who stuck the product in a cabinet never to be used.

Anxiety overtakes them as reality sets in. They must do the one thing that scares them the most: Sell. I mean really sell; to people who will not accept flaws or poor pitches; to people who do not believe they need the product; to people who require being sold in order to buy. They ask themselves, *Would I buy this product? Really?* The business model invoked their passions, not the product or service. Now the model seems flawed.

Most give up on the dream at this point, laughing it off as just a crazy experiment. Yet, deep scars form on their hearts and serve as stark reminders to never try this crazy stunt again. Some of them go even further, joining the ranks of critics crowded around the club entrance, discouraging and berating others. Not once did they consider maybe they picked the wrong business and could succeed at something more suited to their natural skills and talents.

Everyone succeeds in The Lobby at first, and fails to recognize this stage for what it is—the beginning of a long and arduous journey. The relative ease of this phase creates nostalgia and delusions, so it is important new entrepreneurs are especially careful with regard to certain activities, while using their energy on more fruitful tasks. The following sections explain what should be avoided and where to put one's maximum effort while moving through The Lobby.

BEWARE OF HIRING AND FINANCING DECISIONS

Entrepreneurs in this early phase have a sense of invincibility—of knowing they have something big. This confidence is both beneficial and dangerous, requiring extreme caution. Long-term hiring and financing decisions made at this vulnerable point may prove disastrous because of the founder's lack of objectivity.

This could result in taking on too much financial risk and hiring the wrong types of people. Avoid these subjects altogether if possible or enlist the help of more objective experts.

I have known entrepreneurs who took on massive debt in this phase, overconfident they could pay it back in short order. Had they consulted the advice of an expert, they would have been advised to limit the amount of debt or stay away from it altogether. By debt, I refer to bank debt, not that of outside investors.

The ideal source of funding at this stage is that of outside investors be they friends, family or colleagues. Granted, you may have to ask a large number of people to reach the level of funding you need, but this is far better than placing a stranglehold on your business in the infancy stages. Taking on bank debt at this stage is analogous to attaching an anchor to a speedboat. Just as you attempt to make a much needed sharp maneuver, you realize the burden of the weight. By then, it is too late. More on my personal experience with this in later chapters.

Mind Your Business

By mind your business, I mean your accounting operations and cash flow. While founders work on building buzz, enlisting the help of accounting experts is essential to long-term success. Victory is not just around the corner, despite the thinking of typical entrepreneurs. Inexperienced founders expect finances to be taken care of once cash starts rolling in.

This expert is not the guy at the bank or the person who sells mutual funds, for to them you are no more than a commission. Do not be deceived by rhetoric implying otherwise. The real experts you seek have extensive accounting, tax and bookkeeping skills, preferably with a focus on new business startups. Retain the services of true professionals, not family members who simply "know Excel". Consult with these experts often and listen closely to their advice. Their objective nature brings balance to the overambitious nature of founders.

Do not, under any circumstances attempt to be your own accountant. There is far more to this task than installing QuickBooks and entering check amounts. You need someone who can accurately track income, expenses and keep a watchful eye on cash flow. This person applies the brakes when you insist on visiting that buyer in Paris, when a Skype session will do just fine.

Where to Focus Your Energy

So, what should you be doing if you are not to busy yourself with hiring, accounting or financing issues? The sole focus of the entrepreneur in The Lobby is to get their product or service in the hands of the target market beyond early adopters and easy sells. The excitement and optimism at this stage is real and contagious. People feed off of the energy of enthusiastic entrepreneurs. Use it to help build buzz and interest within the market. Also, use this energy to generate interest among potential investors.

Spend your time networking with the right types of people, which I discuss in more detail in Chapter Ten. The burst of energy and optimism that propels you through The Lobby is precious for one reason–it will soon dissipate. Once this happens, getting people excited will seem more difficult and selling will be even harder. The time to use that energy to is now.

In Hindsight

I distinctly remember going through this stage in one of my companies. We enjoyed the extended success of The Lobby; extended because the success lasted for quite some time. Revenues were higher than ever before and the word was starting to spread about our company. This, at a time when all we sold was service, not any type of physical product. Instead of using this momentum to shout from the mountaintops about our popular services, the focus shifted to hiring and financing decisions based on anticipated "boom."

Although these were big customers who paid well, the results were not due to our direct efforts. Most contracts originated outside of our organization through significant referrals—personal contacts within a large and very well known national computer hardware vendor. All readers would recognize the name right away. Half of the battle was won before we arrived for the meetings because the referral came from a trusted advisor whom the customer dealt with for years. Granted, we still needed to do our part by proving our capabilities, but ask any business and they will admit the hardest part is getting a meeting with decision makers. An eight hundred pound gorilla did this tough job for us. This is an ideal scenario only when executed as part of a larger strategy.

While revenues flood in from these types of customers, the entrepreneur must simultaneously focus attention on the tougher sells within the target market. Use the experience and relationships of the existing customer base as a means of building credibility with potential prospects. All the prospect cares about is the results with those customers, not who introduced you. Use this to your advantage, for revenues from early adopters and well-wishers will start to diminish. The business brought in from the market beyond this group will make up for much of those losses and propel you to the next level of your business. We squandered this excellent opportunity. If you are making this same mistake right now and do not change course, prepare yourself for a more difficult road ahead.

In hindsight, the important tasks of hiring and researching the need for financing could have been delegated to outside experts. Entrepreneurs can accomplish these tasks without hiring full-time, dedicated resources. A number of organizations specialize in providing these services to entrepreneurs of all types, and a simple Internet search will turn up several. A good accountant will have a network of professionals who specialize in a number of the services you require. Therefore, start by finding your accountant using the criteria I mentioned earlier in this chapter.

Our lengthy hiring and financing processes ended, and business continued humming along for some time. Then I noticed something menacing. Not only did I see it, but I also felt it. Our market segments slowly dried up and acquiring new clients seemed harder. Just as it seemed things could not get worse, they did. Budgets got slashed and projects stalled. In order to survive we needed to do something we never did before; pick a new sector and sell into "white space." In sales, the term "white space" refers to customers who never bought your product and possibly never heard of you. We needed to learn to really sell and we needed to learn fast. Not an easy feat for a team of infrastructure engineers. Gone were the bright lights and the fanfare of The Lobby. We were entering a more difficult phase and the worst was yet to come.

Key Take Aways

1. The act of filing the legal paperwork to start a business is a good first step but still a minor one.
2. Understanding the phases of entrepreneurship before proceeding is critical.
3. Everyone experiences early successes due to early adopters, family and friends.
4. New entrepreneurs are too optimistic to make financing decisions and should avoid this subject unless they enlist the help of objective third party experts. Otherwise, there is the risk of taking on more debt than is manageable.
5. The flood of initial business is temporary and should not be used as a gauge for making a host of new hires. Again, seek a third party objective expert.
6. The energy of the new entrepreneur is infectious and should be used primarily to market and generate buzz around the products and services.
7. Find an account and a bookkeeper to manage and keep you informed on the financial status of the company. Do not attempt to do this yourself. Again, your energy is better used at this phase for generating buzz.

3
THE GAUNTLET

Nobody talks of entrepreneurship as survival, but that's exactly what it is.
Anita Roddick—Founder of The Body Shop

The price of membership is steep and this is where payment first becomes due. The level of difficulty and duration of this next phase depends in large part on the maneuvers made in The Lobby. Those who make it this far without running for the exits are startled by the change in the atmosphere. Gone are the bright lights, the handshakes and the congratulations, replaced by fear, uncertainty, darkness and constrained movement. Reality sets in as the inevitable weeding out process commences. This is where the herd begins to thin out and the wannabes scramble for the exits. This I consider the entrepreneur's equivalent of boot camp, where bad ideas and those who poorly execute go to die. This is also where heroes are born. Welcome to The Gauntlet.

I have known a number of people over the years that were convinced they had fresh ideas. Armed with only their idea and a small amount of startup capital, they announced their decision to strike out on their own. The relative ease of starting a business lures many to the doors who do not belong—a classic case of bait and switch. As far as this new entrepreneur is concerned he or she truly belongs, but this sentiment is far from the truth.

Most breeze through The Lobby riding the wings of quick sales and optimism, then get thrust full bore into The Gauntlet where they discover what it really means to be an entrepreneur. Now comes the pain and difficulty of being in business as the "market" of well-wishers and easy targets dries up. Doubts and second guessing dominate as the enormity of the task becomes clear.

Without laying the proper foundation in The Lobby by dogmatically focusing on sales and marketing as well as minding the business, The Gauntlet becomes an even more difficult slog. The deafening sound of the original "buzz" becomes nothing more than a whimper, and people are not as excited about the product or the founders. For the inexperienced entrepreneur this is a terrifying realization and is the source of many sleepless nights.

Many choose to head for the exits at this point, never to return. Others, however, know if they can just make it a little further, they will make it to the other side. Now is the time to pause, look over your shoulder at the exits, which are still not too far off, and make a decision. Do you get out while you can still see light, or do you move further into the uncertain path of The Gauntlet? The choice is between the safety and security of the full-time job, or a tough trek through The Gauntlet in pursuit of The Players Lounge. If you are the adventurous type like me, go ahead and take one last look at the exits, then plant your feet firmly and continue moving forward.

Just like in The Lobby, survival in this phase requires deliberate and sustained effort, focusing attention on specific tasks while going out of the way to avoid others. The following sections detail what to do and what to avoid.

BE MINDFUL OF THOUGHTS AND EMOTIONS

Choose your confidants wisely while in this phase because your mental and emotional state is fragile. Words of discouragement delivered with precision can derail your progress, especially if from someone you know and trust. Avoid the original naysayers, as this is their opportunity to deliver the final blow. Whether intentional or not, they will make you feel like a total failure.

Solitude is not the answer either. Whom you reach out to is what makes the difference. Confide in those who support you and your efforts. Meet with mentors, especially other entrepreneurs for guidance and perspective. They have immense insight into the situation because they too went through it themselves.

While getting pummeled in The Gauntlet, I met with a mentor in his office. The situation was quite dire at the time. My original partner ran for the exits into the warm arms of a full-time job. Revenues were down, we were buried in debt and I was running out of ideas.

In contrast, my mentor ran a successful company with increasing profits year over year. His company resided in a posh office complex with over one hundred employees, including a talented sales staff. His success was like a fine stew well simmered over time—settled and nourishing to all who came near. He did not make a show of phoniness or fake machismo. Success was a basic part of his makeup, having enjoyed it for so long. Even though he showed up to work every day, he did so out of preference, not necessity. The place ran just fine without him.

He explained in vivid detail how his original partner bolted for the exits during his time in The Gauntlet. As if this was not bad enough, he took several thousand dollars with him. Even worse, the ex-partner went to work for their biggest competitor. For the next several minutes, he schooled me on the importance of selecting the right type of partner, which was the inspiration for Chapter Eight of this book.

The contrast between his experience in The Gauntlet and his current success struck me and gave me great hope. Surround yourself with these types of people throughout your life, but especially while muddling your way through The Gauntlet.

Review Goals and Focus on Can Do's

Make sure your actions are in harmony with your goals and objectives. Otherwise, you run the risk of falling into "busy work," attending to insignificant details that do not add value. I detail this destructive behavior in Chapter Nine.

Can do's include: Meeting with past and existing clients, prospecting for new opportunities and exploring additional marketing efforts. If you failed to do this properly in The Lobby, now is the chance to get it right. One common mistake is to focus so intently on new business, that existing and past customers go unnoticed. Maintain good and positive relationships with your clients even if they have not purchased in a while. Far too many sales opportunities are lost because of failure to follow up and keep in touch.

However, do not call on anyone unless your mental state is healthy. If it is a down day, pick yourself up before making contact. People have a way of detecting negative emotions, even over the phone.

Maintain Flexibility

One of the hardest things for an entrepreneur to accept is the possibility his or her idea is a failure. The unfortunate first reaction is to cling to the original product or concept, discounting all constructive criticism, which is an extreme and unhealthy position. Perhaps there is a middle course between the two extremes of going down with the ship and chucking it all.

In our case, we adjusted our delivery model. We introduced products and services to compliment, not replace, our original offerings. Not only did this generate a new level of excitement and enthusiasm, but also opened our eyes to additional possibilities. One good idea often leads to several others, especially when working within a group. This injects hope into the business and focuses attention on productive solutions.

Recall Past Triumphs

Form the habit of recalling past triumphs. All of us have faced challenges that seemed impossible to overcome. Yet, we managed to prevail nonetheless. Spend a small amount of time each day reliving some of these moments. I share a couple of my own in the Epilogue. We are not defined or valued by our current circumstances and this is an excellent way to reinforce this truth.

I do not advocate spending hours daydreaming, which is another form of "busy work" and a cheap way of escaping problems. As much as you need to focus on solutions and progress, sometimes it is downright difficult. The purpose of this exercise is to keep a healthy perspective, and prevent your imagination from drifting off into doomsday scenarios. Our visions of disaster are often far worse than reality anyhow.

Once you find yourself in a much better state, immediately turn your attention to the can do's. Do not hesitate for a moment. If you slip back into destructive thinking, revisit past victories once again. Repeat this process as much as necessary to keep your mind off of your fears. Soon, this more productive thought process forms a habit.

Training Camp

Those who survive The Gauntlet will never be the same. They realize strengths and talents they never knew they had. The Gauntlet strengthens your ability to soldier on in the face of adversity and seemingly insurmountable odds. Each tiny victory increases your confidence, courage and sense of self worth. This is something only understood through direct experience.

There is no set time limit on The Gauntlet but there are hopeful signs that relief is near. The trick is knowing where one ends and the other begins, as the line between the two is razor thin. Chapter Four identifies these signs and the steps for capitalizing on them in order to reach The Players Lounge.

In Hindsight

We went wrong by making a common mistake. We attempted to grow a business based off of referrals and sales efforts of people outside of our organization. Also, we focused too much on perfecting our services instead of leaping out of the gate like thoroughbreds.

Sales and marketing are the most important tasks of the beginning entrepreneur. Even our first employee was a technical resource instead of a salesperson, though my gut said to go for the salesperson. This was a horrible miscalculation; one I see new entrepreneurs make quite often.

To minimize the impact of The Gauntlet get out of your comfort zone early. Hit The Lobby with a full sprint toward your target market, not the easy sales that will not last. The market I speak of does not include friends, family, former colleagues or customers poached from previous employers.

Family and friends play an important role with their support and encouragement. Accept the support and take their money if they buy from you. However, do not expect to be the next hotshot entrepreneur because your mom and dad bought your product.

Take this book for example. A number of my close friends and family sent positive comments after reading the sample content I made available on Facebook. Most of them will buy the book to support me and because they want to see me succeed. I suspect they will enjoy the book because it is about someone close to them. However, only a tiny percentage of them fall into my target market and would go looking for this type of book in a bookstore. To make sales projections based on this feedback would be a serious, yet common error.

If you are sitting back wondering what has gone wrong, take a hard look at your customer base. What percentage of them truly falls into your target? How many were poached from your previous employer? How many did you acquire by true business development and prospecting? Now is your opportunity to turn this around. Even in The Gauntlet, this can be fixed so long as you have a good product or service. Chapter Five addresses in more detail the steps for turning things around.

Key Take Aways

1. Preparation for The Gauntlet starts in The Lobby by having a direct, internal sales effort, getting outside help to mind finances, and focusing on your target market.
2. Your market does not include friends, family and former colleagues.
3. Avoid negative personalities and naysayers while in The Gauntlet. Do not share your situation with them, especially if they are close to you.
4. Seek advice from successful mentors and entrepreneurs who experienced The Gauntlet.
5. Focus your efforts on the can do's of the problem, even if the tasks seem tiny.
6. Spend a small amount of time each day reliving past victories, but do not let this turn into daydreaming.
7. Maintain flexibility and keep an eye out for opportunities to enhance or tweak your offerings.
8. Stay in regular contact with past and existing customers.

4
THE PLAYERS LOUNGE

The ultimate measure of a man is not where he stands in moments of comfort, but where he stands at times of challenge and controversy.

Dr. Martin Luther King, Jr.—

The *Players* Lounge? Many will wonder why I chose the word "Player" to define this stage. I personally deplore this term when used to describe a man who "plays" women, a womanizer. Unfortunately, this is a popular term in my own community and young men often greet each other with, "What's up playa?"

One of the definitions by Webster's is: *One actively involved, especially in a competitive field or process: Participant.*

One of my goals is to one day enter a room full of young men and women and greet them as Players. However, my reference will be for a different kind of group—entrepreneurs who have mastered the game of entrepreneurship.

The occupants of the Players Lounge not only play the sport of entrepreneurship, but are masters of the game. How do we identify Players—by revenues and profits? No, we identify them by their station in the venture. The Player is one whose business outgrows him or her to such a degree that personal involvement is no longer required. If they involve themselves in core creative or technical functions, this is out of preference, not necessity. Ask yourself the following question: If you die tomorrow, can your business go on without you? If your answer is no, then you are not a Player.

Let me again draw your attention to the mentor I mentioned in the last chapter. He runs a successful mortgage company but has never written a mortgage in his life. Spend a little time in his office and it becomes clear that his presence is not essential. He does play an important role in terms of guidance, vision and direction, but if he walked out tomorrow for good, things would hum right along without him. This is a clear indicator of success.

The Lobby and The Gauntlet on the other hand, require direct involvement from the founders. The premature withdrawal of a founding member with a key skill set could spell the end, which is why choosing the right partner is essential to success.

In reality, we need an entire book to cover the rewards and challenges of the Players Lounge. In many ways this phase is more challenging than The Gauntlet because the stakes are much higher. However, Players have at their disposal a wide array of resources, tools and, most importantly, experience to get them through rough passages. For now, let us focus on signs of approaching the Players Lounge and how to interact with Players when you meet them—and you will meet them if you traverse The Gauntlet properly. As you near the end of The Gauntlet and close in on the Players Lounge, established Players will find you and help you the rest of the way.

Are We There Yet?

As you go through the most difficult trials of The Gauntlet, two contradictory worlds emerge—one where the walls seem to be caving in and another where you sense a shift in momentum. Perhaps sales are not great but for the first time in a long time, the atmosphere is different. There is an air of excitement again as you get face time with those in your target market beyond the easy wins and early adopters. There is a slight uptick of sales within this group along with buzz and recognition. All signs point to an impending breakthrough just around the corner. There is a sense of getting back to your feet in The Gauntlet after crawling on your knees and barely inching forward. Once back to your feet, you steadily inch forward—first with tiny steps, then with bigger strides. The path is still dark and uncertain but at least there is measurable progress. You make it far enough to sense The Players Lounge, but not quite well enough to see it.

More important is the type of attention coming your way. You find yourself encountering The Players and developing meaningful relationships with them. This contact is not the type established during bland networking events or in online forums. The Players themselves find you, invite you into the inner circle and extend a helping hand in the form of aid and mentorship. This is no accident as it is due to your relentless efforts. Too often, we are so caught up in the day to day of our own worlds that we fail to see the impact of our actions. We may not see the effects but others do and this is the source of breakthroughs.

Players recognize you as one of their own when you meet, so they extend a hand to help you the rest of the way. You may question why someone at a Player level would show such interest, as you still feel so close to failure. I experienced this myself while sitting in a mentor's office. A mutual friend introduced us, and we connected right away. I sat in his office for a couple of hours taking in his wisdom and advice. He saw something in me at the time that I honestly could not see because The Gauntlet was bearing down on me. He said something that day that I will never forget: "I think you have potential and I want to help you." At the time, we had known each other for only a couple of days.

Somehow, this group of master entrepreneurs notices all of your efforts, struggles and potential, and you begin to attract them. At first, you will feel uncomfortable in their company because you question if you really belong with them, for clearly they have made it and you can barely pay your bills. Do your best to resist this destructive thinking and see yourself just as The Players see you. Just as in The Lobby and the early stages of The Gauntlet, you must focus your efforts on specific actions.

ROLLING WITH THE PLAYERS

When in their company, pay close attention to all of their advice even if you do not understand everything. Do not hesitate to ask lots of questions, as they are eager to provide answers. They have gone through all that you have and far worse in most cases.

A word of caution here—be authentic. One reason Players are successful is their ability to size up people and situations quickly. The moment they suspect you as an inauthentic "schmoozer," they will distance themselves. Do not attempt to impress them with unwarranted compliments or other forms of flattery. Also, do not come across as desperate or weak as these are states of mind incompatible with success. They disdain this type of character as much as you do. Remember, no one likes a loser and will not be willing to help one.

Along with helpful advice, The Players will offer to make introductions to others who can be helpful. This includes potential customers, strategic partners and business influencers. Take them up on this offer without hesitation. The Players wield considerable influence, and their opinions carry a lot of weight with those within their circles. You will be expected to act swiftly, so be prepared to do so.

FINANCIAL SUPPORT

In rare instances, The Players will offer financial support in the form of loans, investments or access to investors. My case was something quite different and still astounds me to this day. One day I awoke unsure how certain bills would get paid. The day ended with a $50,000 commitment from a mentor, $15,000 advanced that very day.

Here is the story. A recent attempt to raise capital fell through, so the mentor called me to his office for a meeting. In the meeting, he asked me how much I would need up front if he made $50,000 available to me. I hesitated as it sounded too much like charity, and I was no charity case. The mentor chuckled a bit and rephrased the question. He asked how much I would withdraw if I had a line of credit with his company. I told him $15,000. He promptly wrote me a check and sent me on my way. This guy trusted me. An excellent reader of people and one who had learned to trust his gut, he did not hesitate to act once the course of action was clear.

When things like this happen, understand that even if you are not in The Players Lounge, you probably have the make of a Player. The Players who reach out to you see something but you have to learn to see the same in yourself.

BE READY TO DELIVER

When The Players arrive to offer their help, they will want something in return, so be prepared to deliver. However, do not make promises you are not able to keep. This is the surest way of losing favor with them. Your part will likely be in the form of offering your product or service at a discounted rate to them or their key contacts. This is a perfect opportunity for you to highlight your product or service, so be as serious as if you were dealing with a new customer. Players are where they are because of hard work and dedication. Their interest is in helping you reach the same level, not supporting you like a needy nephew.

What they want in return more than anything is for you to be exactly what they believe you to be. They have stellar reputations, which is why their recommendations carry such value. Do not make them look bad by failing to perform when they grant you opportunities. When you showcase your product or service, make this the best performance of your life. When they put you in front of investors, make it your best presentation ever. Do not ever put them in the uncomfortable position of having to apologize for you. Word will spread quickly in their circles that you are not one to be taken seriously.

FROM THE GAUNTLET TO THE PLAYERS LOUNGE

If you make it this far and you have a great product or service, growth is not too far off. As you sign more of your target market and sales increase, take the time to scrutinize your team and fill in the gaps where you can. You want to get to the point where you are no longer in the business. This is where so many entrepreneurs go wrong. Just as things start turning around, they fail once again to make the transition from specialist to entrepreneur. They go right back to some of their original mistakes, risking a long descent back into The Gauntlet. This is the make or break point where the entrepreneur must decide to grow into a Player by rounding out the team or remain stagnant and eventually regress.

Ensure there is a plan to build out your management team to support growth. Determine the milestones and track them closely. When will you add the next salesperson? When do you add the sales manager? When do you hire operations and business managers? Each team member should shore up a weakness in the current team.

Steady growth requires delegation of core product and service functions, preferably to people far smarter than you. This means moving further away from the action on the field—the day to day, into more of an overarching leadership role. For example, if you are an engineer and do not delegate engineering tasks to other engineers as your business grows, your success will be short-lived and you will miss The Players Lounge by a hair. This is the difference between growing a job and growing a business.

This is also the time to take a shot at raising capital from angels or other private investors. You can undoubtedly illustrate an uptick in business and positive sales projections. With the return of enthusiasm and excitement, this is the ideal time to talk to anyone in the position to help. Tap the newly built network of influencers brought on by The Players. However, this does not include approaching banks. I will explain why in Chapter Six.

Acceptable Stagnation

A space exists between the depths of The Gauntlet and The Players Lounge where revenues are steady but the organization does not reach the level of the Players. Is it possible to operate in this space and achieve long-term success? This all depends on how one defines success. Success in entrepreneurship expands on our field of choices, allowing us to remain in our businesses out of sheer enjoyment, not necessity. I see this as the ultimate victory—doing what you love because you want to, not because you need to pay the bills. Some, however, choose to remain in a state of "acceptable stagnation"—a business which is no more than a long-term, steady, self-made job. They retain a group of regular, well-paying clients and do not concern themselves with growth. The primary focus is maintaining a certain lifestyle and income level, while doing the work they love. Most refer to this model as lifestyle entrepreneurship—an acceptable approach so long as the entrepreneur understands this choice and builds the appropriate strategy.

This group experiences modest growth, which is mostly organic—the result of referrals from a small stable of loyal customers. The key for them is a committed client base that buys often, pays on time and purchases in large amounts. If overwhelmed by too much work, they either subcontract to other lifestyle entrepreneurs or refuse to take on additional business altogether.

What differentiates this group from the uninformed specialists described in earlier chapters? Successful lifestyle entrepreneurs understand and accept the role of entrepreneur, but make a conscious decision to limit growth. They breeze through The Lobby, fight their way through The Gauntlet and learn all the lessons along the way just like everyone else, but ascension into The Players Lounge is far more work than they wish to take on. Once they reach the threshold between The Gauntlet and The Players lounge, they opt for a strategy that maintains the business at an acceptable level but goes no further. Again, this is a conscious decision with a deliberate strategy.

This approach to entrepreneurship carries greater risk because of limited choices during difficult periods. Unlike those in The Players Lounge for example, lifestyle entrepreneurs cannot withstand extended downturns in the economy or radical changes to their industries. Whereas Players can shed resources and reorganize, lifestyle entrepreneurs could be forced to shut down, collaborate with others to survive or introduce additional products and services. In other words, they may be forced into a form of entrepreneurship they chose to avoid all along.

In Hindsight

One day I sat at my desk and calculated the amount of revenue we could generate by me returning to project work. At the time we had subcontractors and employees in the field bringing in revenues and seemed illogical not to tap my own skills to add to the pot. This approach was both wrongheaded and shortsighted, for as I buried my head in technology, no one minded the store so to speak. Although we chose a long-term strategy to replace my technical skills, we failed to do so in search of short term gains.

I missed another golden opportunity to further replace myself as advised earlier in this chapter. A large project requiring my specific skills came up. Others on the team could have done the job with some assistance from me, but I had the most experience. Taking on this large project killed what little progress we had made in the areas of sales and marketing. After being preoccupied with hiring and financing, I then shifted to a nine month long technical project. Instead of delegating, I decided to do it all myself, and it needed to be perfect.

As this project concluded, another came up requiring the same skills. Again, I took it on myself instead of delegating to others. Instead of positioning myself to be out of the business, I became further entrenched. Without my direct involvement, a significant portion of revenues would be impacted. Blinded by shortsighted dollar signs instead of long term strategic thinking, we were slowly killing our business.

The goal was not lifestyle entrepreneurship. Building a business worth selling for a profit was the objective. Instead, we made this critical strategic error, which we would live to regret.

Key Take Aways

1. A Player is one whose business can function without him. Direct involvement is often by choice, not necessity.
2. It is normal to live in contradictory worlds as you approach The Players Lounge—one in which the

walls are crumbling down and another where a breakthrough seems right around the corner.
3. Look for an uptick in sales and recognition within your target market.
4. Players will take notice and offer assistance but will expect something in return. Be willing and able to deliver what is requested.
5. Do not be afraid to ask lots of questions. Players are eager to help and to see you succeed.
6. Do not come across as desperate or weak when dealing with Players. This will turn them off and make them less willing to help you.
7. Be authentic. Do not attempt to "schmooze" Players as they consider this deplorable. They are skilled at detecting inauthentic types.
8. Be prepared for meetings with the contacts of Players. They could be potential customers, investors or other key decision-makers.
9. The best you can do is performing at your peak when introduced to a Player's contacts. Do not cause them embarrassment or regret.
10. Lifestyle entrepreneurship is acceptable in terms of building a job for yourself but carries greater risks during difficult times.
11. Successful lifestyle entrepreneurs make this choice consciously and build a workable strategy. Other specialists simply fail to make the transition to entrepreneur.

5
SELL! SELL! SELL!

The key to evangelism is a great product. It is easy, almost unavoidable, to catalyze evangelism for a great product. It is hard, almost impossible, to catalyze evangelism for crap.

Guy Kawasaki—

What is the most important job of a new entrepreneur? For fun, I asked a new entrepreneur this question and gave him three chances to answer correctly. He gave typical answers he read in many books:

- Create the vision.
- Build the enterprise and structure.
- I don't remember the third answer but it was just as lofty and pointless as the first two.

Too often, we go out of our way to complicate things that require no complexity, and nothing is complex about the answer to this question. The most pressing responsibility of the new entrepreneur is to SELL! SELL! SELL! Bookstores abound with countless works on the science and art of selling, but entrepreneurs blow past them in favor of "business" books or the biographies of legendary leaders. Many of these books adorn the bookshelf in my office: "Good to Great," "Pour Your Heart Into It," "The 7 Habits of Highly Effective People." The business section is where we belong because we are "business people", not sales people, so the logic goes.

I learned many lessons from these and similar books, but many of the books entrepreneurs love so much gloss over the importance of selling. To embrace and become comfortable with the sales process is not only the smart thing to do, but also an absolute necessity.

"I am not a salesperson," insists the entrepreneur.

"I am an engineer."

"A developer."

"An accountant."

"A *fill in the blank*."

This is a bitter pill to swallow, but an entrepreneur without the capacity or willingness to market and sell is nothing more than a soon-to-be-unemployed specialist. The most groundbreaking product in the world is useless if no one knows of its existence. Refusal to accept this reality is the surest path to failure.

A Bold Declaration

Here is a declaration that many of the readers will disagree with: Salespeople are far more valuable and important than the widgets they sell or the engineers who design them. Go back and read the previous sentence again for it is one of the most important points in this book. For you engineers and techies who take extreme "umbrage" to such a ludicrous statement, I will prove it. A skilled salesperson can sell anything, even a mediocre product. Verify this for yourself by examining some of the crappy products on the market today. A person who knows how to generate buzz and interest in a product or service can make a living just about anywhere. Place that person in the middle of a crowd and watch them work their magic.

In sharp contrast, a genius engineer with the greatest widget ever, will never make it out of his garage unless and until he learns how to sell. The engineer needs the salesperson but the salesperson does not need the engineer or the widget. Any product or service will do. A good salesperson can make a living selling fruits and berries if they choose. How many innovative ideas and inventions go undiscovered because some genius refuses to accept the importance of sales and marketing?

DROPPED IN THE MIDDLE OF NOWHERE

To illustrate this further let me share with you a true story. Muslims living in Mecca, Saudi Arabia experienced extreme hardship in the early days of their faith over 1,400 years ago. The conflict between the small band of worshippers and the elites of Mecca reached its pinnacle, forcing the Muslims to flee for their lives. They left only with what they could carry, leaving behind their homes, property, families and businesses. Some of them were wealthy and fled with nothing.

The refugees were later accepted into the neighboring city of Medina where the townspeople were hospitable and accommodating. A wealthy inhabitant of Medina named Saad ibn Ar-Rabiah offered one of the refugees, Abdul-Rahman ibn Awf, half of his wealth to give him a fresh start in the new town. Ibn Awf refused and simply asked for directions to the marketplace where locals and travelers engaged in trade around the clock. Once he found the marketplace, he went right into the business of trading. Ibn Awf lived a life of luxury as a wealthy merchant in Mecca and was confident in his ability to rebuild his fortune from nothing. Within a few months of arriving with only the clothes on his back, this refugee was wealthy once again. Like all successful entrepreneurs, he understood the business of selling. He did not concern himself with what to sell. He did not have to build or design anything. He simply needed access to people with something to trade.

Marketing Plan, Not Business Plan

Comprehensive business plans take a lot of time and effort to write, which is why so many new entrepreneurs put off writing them. All the while the perceived necessity for this seventy-five-page monstrosity haunts them. Let go the anxiety of not wanting to write a business plan because you do not need one. Business plans are for banks and investors, who are not interested in you if you are not already making money or have some sort of breakthrough technology. This is especially true for banks. Even in my discussions with venture capitalists, if you get them interested in your product or service, they care about only one other thing–how does this make money?

So save yourself a lot of anguish and focus on creating a marketing plan, which should answer three basic questions:

- Who is your market?
- How will you reach them?
- How much will you charge them?

If you have not given this topic a great deal of thought, make it the very next thing you do when you finish this chapter.

THE SCIENCE OF SELLING

You will not find the "hows" of selling in this book as plenty of books on the market cover this topic far better than I can. My goal is to convince you of the importance of making sales your number one priority. Without first understanding and enthusiastically embracing this task, discussions on the hows are pointless.

A favorite book of mine on the topic of selling is "Customer Centric Selling" by Michael T. Bosworth. The book focuses on technology-based sales but is appropriate for all fields. Do yourself a favor, take a trip down that aisle in the bookstore marked SALES, and add this book to your library, as the success of your business depends on it.

A LESSON IN ZEALOTRY

What if you discovered the cure for cancer and could save millions of lives? Would it not be your moral responsibility to tell anyone and everyone willing to listen? Would you take the responsibility lightly? Would you leave it to others to take on the responsibility for you? How far would you go to spread the word? Now for the most important question: What do we call the process of spreading the word about your cure? We call this selling.

Given enough passion and belief, people enter the mode of SELL, SELL, SELL without realizing. This also happens to entrepreneurs who passionately believe in their product or service. I do not mean wild enthusiasm but focused and disciplined thought that goes into formulating a sound marketing and sales plan.

If you have a useful service or product that can improve the lives of those in your target market, are you not obligated to get it in their hands? Granted, you do not have the cure for cancer but maybe you can help businesses save millions in lost productivity. Perhaps it improves the quality of life for families, children or couples. Maybe it allows people to temporarily escape reality and enjoy life for a few moments a day. Regardless of the product or service, if it has the potential to add to the quality of life in even the slightest manner, you owe it to your target market to get it in their hands. If it is not compelling enough to invoke this level of passion, you are either in the wrong business or have the wrong product.

Entrepreneurs can learn a lot about selling from religious zealots. Look at the guy who stands on a street corner for hours selling his organization's newspapers. Then we have those who spend hours canvassing neighborhoods on weekends, going door-to-door "selling" their religion. Most people will not answer the door and those who do will show little interest in the peddler's "product." Yet, they keep on going from door to door, day after day, week after week, year after year. Their belief and passion is what drives them. Are these neighborhood canvassers salespeople? Absolutely. Without this type of religious-type fervor, you may as well pack it up and go home, for you have a passion deficit.

No Outsourcing Allowed

This brings me to another important point, which is you cannot outsource this responsibility. This must come from within the organization, not from outside. Either the entrepreneur directly or someone from the team must own the task of sales. Collaboration with others is a recommended strategy, but you must not rely on them to do the selling for you. Your products and services are not their chief priority because they have their own. Any company, especially a small one that relies solely on sources outside of their company for sales is doomed.

Show Me the Money

The first time I realized the superiority of the sales process is when I prepared a pitch for a group of venture capitalists. The person who helped me prepare kept drilling me about the sales and marketing plan. Whenever I talked about the technology, he brought the conversation back to sales and marketing. Sure enough, when I pitched to the venture capitalists, the sales process was the first thing they asked about. Who is the market and how do you plan on reaching them? By the way, how much have you sold so far?

To witness this for yourself, take a look at the television program "Shark Tank," where entrepreneurs get the opportunity to pitch to a group of venture capitalists or "sharks." There are countless episodes of enthusiastic entrepreneurs with the latest widget or product. I witnessed episodes where even the venture capitalists seemed genuinely interested in a product until the dreaded question came up—how many have you sold? Entrepreneurs with unflattering sales are often sent packing.

Let me close this subject with another example of the importance of sales in the entrepreneurial landscape. One of my mentors with a multimillion dollar company mentioned something in passing as I left his office one day. I knew there was some significance to his statement but I did not appreciate it at the time. As the saying goes, the teacher arrives only when the student is ready to learn.

He planned to leave for a big vacation the following week. Nothing spectacular here except whom he planned on taking with him. "I'm taking my entire sales team to the Bahamas," he said proudly. He did not say the technical department or administrative staff, but the sales team. The sales department is responsible for the single most important part of any business—revenues. Without them we would have no IBM, no Microsoft, no Dell, and no Apple. Smart corporations and smart entrepreneurs reward salespeople handsomely as they are the lifeblood of the company. For the new entrepreneur the mantra is sell or die.

In Hindsight

By now you know it took a lot of time and many hard lessons before I understood the importance of owning the sales process. Some argue you need a dedicated salesperson only after you hit one million dollars in revenues, but it will take a long time before many entrepreneurs reach this threshold. When we finally decided to hire our first employee, we tried to kill two birds with one stone by hiring a technical resource with an outgoing personality. We thought we could utilize him for both tasks, similar to the way we did with ourselves. This turned out to be a costly error.

We did technical work and sales, but the problem is we gave precedence to technical work. Sales became a priority only when we needed new clients and projects. To make up the difference we relied on referrals from outside affiliates and collaborators, which turned out to be an inadequate strategy as well. In short, the most important task to every entrepreneur ran second fiddle to our fetish for technology. If you are unable or unwilling to own the sales process, be sure to hire someone who will. There are countless salespeople who are willing to work on a commission only basis. Keep in mind, however, they will insist on large commissions.

If you have not addressed this issue thus far, make it the very next thing you do. A salesperson is not a luxury you acquire once you can afford it. They are as much a necessity as the accountant or the bookkeeper, if not more so. If you truly cannot sell, fine. Make it a priority to find someone who can and pay them handsomely once they deliver. Otherwise, it is just a matter of time before you close up shot for good.

There was a time when we did take up this responsibility and performed quite well until we let our fetish for technical services and engineering get in the way. Once the required action was clear, we executed by profiling businesses within our target market and hitting the streets. In one instance we walked in without an appointment and asked to speak to the person in charge of Information Technology. A few minutes later he came out and invited us in. The meeting was brief but effective. The manager wanted to take on a complex project but had no idea where to start. His own investigation had led him down several different paths, each contradicting the other. With the picture he painted, this organization needed a lot of help and we had the expertise to do the job.

We then took to the white board and helped him narrow down the choices. We also explained why the chosen solution would be better suited to his unique needs. The manager asked us to come back with a detailed proposal, and we agreed but with one condition. He would have to bring his boss to the next meeting or no deal. Experience taught us to always make sure all key decision makers are present during proposal meetings. Within a few weeks this prospect was a new customer.

This experience was classic business development to the core—identify the market; determine how to reach them; provide a service at a reasonable, yet profitable price. We also learned that a few good yeses are worth getting a bunch of nos. The response from that customer helped us forget the previous prospects that turned us away. The market responded to our services without being warmed up by an eight hundred pound gorilla with prior history. The sooner new entrepreneurs can get out of their comfort zones and learn this lesson, the easier their journeys will be.

Key Take Aways

1. Start with a marketing plan, not a business plan.
2. Once you become an entrepreneur, you are no longer a specialist. Your primary focus must be on sales and marketing.
3. Do not outsource the responsibility of

marketing and sales. There must be internal accountability for this important task.
4. Start your marketing plan by answering three basic questions—Who is your market? How do you reach them? What do you charge them?
5. Learn to have a level of faith and zealotry in yourself and your products similar to that of religious zealots.
6. If you do not have the right level of faith and passion in your product or service, you may be in the wrong business or have the wrong product.
7. Purchase the book "Customer Centric Selling," by Michael T. Bosworth.

6
IF I HAD A MILLION DOLLARS...

A man in debt is so far a slave.
Ralph Waldo Emerson—

Remember that catchy sing-along by the Bare Naked Ladies, "If I Had A Million Dollars?" The singer goes through a checklist of items he would buy if only he had a cool million. Actually, if he bought everything on the list, he would still have a lot of cash left over! Trust me, I did the math. Like so many others, I like the tune because it is witty and catchy, but it is also a lesson for the observant entrepreneur. Ask any entrepreneur what they need more than anything and most will say cash. This typically means funding from venture capitalists, banks, family members or various forms of angel investors. Cash in whatever form is the oxygen of the entrepreneurial venture. So, if I gave you one million dollars right now, how would you put it to use? How exactly would you invest the funds in the business for the best possible return? If you do not know the answer to this question, you have a big problem. More important than the capital itself is knowing how and where to use it for the best possible results.

I recall having a conversation in my office with an entrepreneur I met at a business conference several months earlier. Let's call him Edward. He owned a successful software development firm in the midst of an expansion phase. A friend of Edward's in Japan wanted to make a large investment in an American company. As far as his friend was concerned anything in America was a good bet, and he offered Edward $600,000 in investment capital. My jaw hit the floor since we were actively seeking funding ourselves. If my jaw dropped from the first comment, I almost fell off of my chair from the next one. Edward told me he declined his friend's offer. I could not believe my ears.

"How can you turn down that kind of money?" I asked him. His answer illustrated a level of maturity I had not reached. He did not know how he would use the money so he decided to decline the offer. I understood him on a gut level, but I still could not imagine turning down $600,000 under any circumstances. This was exactly my problem and the problem of many entrepreneurs.

Money Is Not Your Problem...

No amount of money will save you from yourself if you poorly execute your plan. Money will only mask your mistakes and delay your failure if you lack the fundamentals of running a venture. In the early stages of a business, taking large sums of money regardless of the source is tempting. Exercise discipline and do not accept any funding until you solidify your plans for its use.

This flies in the face of the usual advice, which instructs entrepreneurs to seek funding when they do not need it. The rationale is to hold it in reserve for the rainy days that will eventually come. It is not that I totally disagree with this view, but determining exactly how to manage the funds and when to use them is an important detail too often overlooked. Work out these details before seeking capital and avoid "just in case" funding.

...And the Bank Is Not Your Friend

Stay away from banks in the early days of your venture. Those who attempt to build a business on bank debt could face a more difficult future as they make their way through The Gauntlet. Howard Shultz, CEO of Starbucks, addressed this point in his book "Pour Your Heart into It." He said the following:

"Another important thing I learned during that difficult time was that taking on debt is not the best way to fund a company. Many entrepreneurs prefer borrowing money from banks because doing so allows them to keep control in their own hands. They fear that raising equity by selling shares will mean a loss of personal control over the operation. I believe that the best way for an entrepreneur to maintain control is by performing well and pleasing shareholders, even if his or her stake is below fifty percent. That risk is far preferable to the danger of heavy debt, which can limit the possibilities for future growth and innovation."

Another reason to avoid banks in the early stages is the lack of experience negotiating at this level. Negotiations must always be done from a position of strength, which most new business owners lack in the early phases of their ventures. Too often entrepreneurs are so happy someone is willing to give them money, they agree to almost anything. We fell into this trap ourselves, and it turned into one of the worst decisions we ever made.

NEGOTIATING FROM A POSITION OF WEAKNESS

Times were good as we breezed through The Lobby enjoying one success after another. We were so busy with multiple projects and customers that we hired our first employee. We sought out capital with only a vague idea of how we would use it, but wanted it "just in case." The bank was satisfied with our cash flow and impressive stable of clients. This included existing contracts, purchase orders and invoices totaling more than $1,000,000.

Banks are notoriously risk averse and this one wanted far more guarantees than we expected. As a veteran of Desert Storm, I qualified for the Small Business Administration's Patriot Express loan program. The SBA guarantees the loan in the event the borrower defaults. The bank approved us for the amount we requested, and we jumped at the opportunity. However, we were not negotiating from a position of strength as we were just happy to be at the table. Like so many at this stage, we believed the bank did us a favor, while in reality we were the customer, not the other way around.

A couple things I considered strange occurred during these "negotiations" which did not feel right in my gut. First, as a condition of the contract, we had to move all of our business banking to the new bank. Any accounts with other banks were a violation of our contract. Second, the closing documents arrived in the mail with additional provisions regarding collateral. In addition to both founders' homes as collateral, they also required the following:

1. Existing and future receivables
2. All existing company assets

3. All FUTURE company assets.

This last one seemed especially odd and my gut senses were in overdrive. Anything the company acquired during the course of the loan automatically would become collateral. Though I will not disclose the exact loan amount (this is one of the arguments my wife won during the editing process), I can tell you it was far less than $100,000. Half of the amount was a term loan and the other half a line of credit.

In addition, we needed permission and a written justification each time we needed to access the line of credit. This added significant delays when making purchases for resell purposes. Many experts and entrepreneurs we consulted with long after the fact found the terms uncharacteristically restrictive. We had no business negotiating this loan on our own, which in reality was not a negotiation at all.

Compare this to the relationship we had with our previous bank. They also gave us a generous credit line but required only our receivables as collateral. We could use the funds as we needed without additional permission or paperwork, and we could open other bank accounts wherever we chose. Another key difference is the way we were treated. This bank came across as genuinely interested in our business and serving us. When we closed the account, the bank went out of their way to keep us, but our agreement with the new bank prevented us from having accounts with any other banks.

You may ask then why we bothered to switch. We anticipated growth and wanted access to a larger amount, and the SBA's Patriot Express loan program seemed a perfect fit. However, our previous bank did not participate in the SBA's program. They assured us they planned on partnering with the SBA on the program but we were impatient. In hindsight, we were blinded by cash, and unwittingly attached an anchor to our speedboat.

NEGOTIATING FROM A POSITION OF STRENGTH

The person writing this book knows better and is better suited to be at the negotiating table. To negotiate from a position of strength does not mean the odds are always in your favor. It means possessing enough self respect and personal value for yourself so as not to take just any offer. You let the party across the table understand you do not have to do business on their terms, even if they hold something you want. Players know to shop the loan, have a lawyer review the paperwork and pass up any offer they do not find agreeable. For a text book example on dealing with banks in the correct manner, see Chapter Thirteen of "Pour Your Heart Into It" by Howard Shultz and Dori Jones Yang. From pages 183 – 184 they describe the "beauty contest" Starbucks management put investment banks through in order to win the opportunity to handle the upcoming IPO or Initial Public Offering. They go on to describe a large investment bank that arrived in a stretch limousine to give a presentation. This group made no efforts to visit the roasting facilities or to really learn the business. The attitude was Starbucks was lucky to have such a prestigious bank willing to talk to them. It should come as no surprise that Starbucks rejected the proposal.

Okay, so you are not a billion dollar company on the eve of your big IPO, but the same rule applies. Any bank that makes you feel you are the lucky one for having the opportunity to sit at their table is not a bank you want

Presidents, Pilots & ENTREPRENEURS

to do business with. If you have a model that is working and profitable, there are a number of institutions that would love to have you as a client. Make them earn your business, just like you must work to earn the business of your own customers.

We made that deal in The Lobby, but now we were in The Gauntlet. Times were difficult and we had not paid down our credit line in the agreed upon period of one year. Many banks, including our previous bank, have this as a requirement for business lines of credit. The credit line must be zeroed out by the end of the year but ours carried a balance. Revenues had gone south, and we were fighting for our survival.

I spent countless hours on the phone trying to convince the bank to agree to some sort of payment plan, but they would not budge. Attempts to get the amount refinanced by other institutions were unsuccessful as anything we could use as collateral was tied up in this agreement. After several months of stalemate, phone calls and threats, the bank requested a meeting at the branch. My goal for this meeting was to negotiate a deal with the bank that would allow us to pay down the line with regular monthly payments similar to the term loan, giving us enough time to get our revenues in order and pay down the line completely. Most would say I was in no position to negotiate, but entrepreneurs must believe there is always room to negotiate.

Meet The Hammer

Up until this time, all meetings were held in my office and were between just myself and our direct representative who was basically a salesperson. This time it would be with a guy I nicknamed "The

Hammer." I was warned The Hammer was not in business development, but was instead "all about protecting the interests of the bank." This is the person who is responsible for frightening entrepreneurs when they fall behind in their payments.

I did my homework before this meeting by contacting the SBA about my situation with the bank. They provided me with an abundance of information that proved helpful in the meeting. A mentor with years of experience in dealing with banks also gave me helpful advice and negotiating tips. Remember to do extensive research before entering any negotiation, especially in cases where the other party wants you to believe they have the advantage.

When I arrived at the branch, my sales representative greeted me with a handshake and led me to a small conference room. We exchanged some pleasantries before he left to find The Hammer. The bank branch was surprisingly small, not much bigger than some of the small offices in my own office building. I remember being very unimpressed with the place, which may have helped me psychologically.

As I sat at the conference table waiting for the two of them to arrive, I was calm and confident. In my mind, we were all professionals, and I expected the meeting to be conducted as such. To break the ice I decided I would greet The Hammer with a warm smile and a light joke. I would say, "It's very nice of you to call me here to offer me more money." This is exactly what I did when the two of them entered the room, but The Hammer was not amused. He made it clear with a tinge of hostility in his voice that he did not call me in for this reason and the matter was quite serious. I was taken aback by his antagonistic tone, and I am sure I looked genuinely surprised.

The best thing I can do at this point is to take you there instead of trying to describe it further. The following is a portion of a word-for-word transcription of the meeting. I plan on making the full conversation available on this book's companion blog at:

www.PresidentsPilotsEntrepreneurs.com.

I have changed names, dates and places to "protect the innocent" so to speak. I am also considering releasing the full audio of the meeting and making it available for download from the blog site. Even my wife believes I've exposed too much, but my goal is to help as many entrepreneurs as I can.

Me: "I'm sure this isn't the only conversation you've had like this as of late. But what I am offering at this point is to re-amortize the loan, term it out and let's come up with a reasonable payment that I can actually afford so that I can get this credit line paid off. Whether we make it a five-year term, a three-year term—I did do some research on the Patriot Express. Within the manual it actually says you can do that for up to three years or up to 120 months. That is an option."

The Hammer: "That can only happen if there is a means to support for repayment."

Me: "There is a means. It comes down to what the payment is. What I can actually afford."

The Hammer to Sales Rep: "Do you have anything that actually shows that?"

Sales Rep: "We do but it doesn't support additional payments. It shows a salary and a debt load. It does not show the ability to add on debt."

The Hammer to Sales Rep: "Does it show the ability to make the payments he currently has?"

Sales Rep: "Correct."

The Hammer to Sales Rep: "Does it show that?"

Sales Re: "No. No it does not."

The Hammer to Me: "So we are amortizing something out that you cannot afford."

Me: "But I have a contract right now with (undisclosed) and we are still waiting on the first invoice payment on that. The first invoice is (undisclosed). The next invoice is (undisclosed). And each invoice is worth a certain amount up to a total of (undisclosed). Out of those amounts I'm pretty sure we can come up with some kind of payment structure that I can afford. I find it very difficult to believe that we are in such a bad situation that—"

The Hammer: "You are in a bad situation." That's why you're talking to me."

Me: "What I said was I find it hard to believe that we are in such a bad situation that we cannot come up with some kind of reasonable payment plan for me to pay you guys off and for me to stay in business. Now you probably don't care about any of this other stuff that I'm about to say, which is fine. However, right now, and I have communication with the second guy in command at (undisclosed). The only person higher is (undisclosed). We have a contract bid right now with (undisclosed) and (undisclosed) for a contract bid for one billion dollars. That's billion with a B, for the (undisclosed). It is down to two companies. Right now there is a big political fight going on. I just had the conversation with (undisclosed) two weeks ago. He said to me, 'Look. It's a lot of money and people are fighting over it. It would have been settled if it were not for the politics behind it. Our lobbyist is there. Their lobbyist is there and everyone is fighting over this thing. But it's going to come through and when it does, we're all going to do extremely well.' That's one item, and I feel extremely confident in that."

The Hammer: "Well, you know—"

Me: "Let me finish. You have to let me finish."

The Hammer: "I can let you finish but what you're talking about is futures and maybes and, and, and, and somewhere down the lines..."

Me: "I'm not talking about futures and maybes. What's happening today is I have an (undisclosed) invoice out right now to the (undisclosed) for our first payment. The payment should be—"

The Hammer: "And what debts do you have against that?"

Me: "Excuse me?"

The Hammer: "What debts do you have against that (undisclosed)? What debts do you have?

Me: "What debts do I have?" Sigh.

The Hammer: "No, you pull out (undisclosed salary amount)."

Me: "From where?"

The Hammer to Sales Rep: "Doesn't he pull out (undisclosed salary amount)?"

Sales Rep: "That's been about the average amount."

The Hammer: "But that was your salary when you were pulling (undisclosed amount). And now it is still your salary when you are only pulling (undisclosed amount).

Me: "But what I'm saying to you is—"

The Hammer: "Yeah but what I'm saying to you is if you're making (undisclosed amount), you've not down-scaled your salary with your sales. "

Me: "My salary has been down-scaled. I do not make the same amount of money today that I made when we first opened this loan. I don't. I mean that's just the truth. And I think the numbers support that. You don't have to accept it."

The Hammer: "Okay."

Me: "Now can I add the next bit of information that you probably don't care about because it is just maybes and probablys? But for someone like me, maybes and probablys are important because it's part of business. The next maybe slash probably, as you term it unfortunately, is a joint marketing effort we have with (undisclosed multinational company) right now. I have a sales call coming up with their entire regional sales team. We are the only partner in the region certified to offer this solution. The only one. The only one. And off of that we have pending, right now, with (undisclosed large customer) to open up this solution to the entire region. So yes, it's in my best interest and yours for me to stay in business."

The Hammer: "Naah. It's, it's in your best interest to, uh … we are at a point where we've been. How many extensions (directed to sales rep)?"

Sales Rep: "Um. I have to look at it. Over a year and a half now."

The Hammer: "I mean, this conversation is a long time coming."

Me: "Maybe we should have had it sooner. We probably should have had this conversation eight months ago. Alright?"

The Hammer: "Yeah. You've got to understand that we're at a point where–what's your plan to pay us off?"

Me: "Well, as I just said, and this is coming from my discussion with the SBA and folks who run the Patriot Express loan program, as well as the information that's in the handbook."

The Hammer: "Um hm."

Me: "This is a solution if you are willing to—"

The Hammer: "There's nothing wrong with us being willing. Where's the money that's going to pay?"

Me (chucking a bit): "As I said already we have a project with (undisclosed). We have another project coming up with (undisclosed)."

The Hammer: "You have to show us out of each one of those where the money's going to come from."

Me: "Then, that's what we need to settle. How much of a monthly payment can my company afford to pay down this line of credit that is going to be termed out? So, I can't borrow against it anyway. I don't want to borrow against it anymore at this point and I'm sure you wouldn't let me anyway. But the point is, come up with something reasonable that I can actually pay…"

The Hammer: "Do you have a business office? Somebody in…you're sales. Do you have somebody that runs your business office?"

Me: "Well, I'm sales and engineering but okay. Uh …"

The Hammer: "You can be engineering too, but do you have a business office person? Someone that does your books and says, 'What are you doing?' (he laughs a bit). Someone who says, 'We only have this much money…'"

Me: "Is that a joke or is that a serious question?"

The Hammer: "It's not a joke. That's a serious thing."

Me: "Okay."

The Hammer: "Entrepreneurs that are sales, that are spending all of their time building their business, don't pay attention to the finance back—"

Me: "Alright, so let me ask you a question—"

The Hammer: "No wait. Let me finish what I'm saying."

Me: "Oh, I thought that was a question."

The Hammer: "The seriousness is that, is that it's hard for us to buy into something that we've not seen materialize in over a year."

Me: "So let me answer your question. Yes, I have two things. I have someone who handles the books. Secondly, I have another person who has a master's degree in accounting who has come on to help deal with more of the financial perspectives as well as the financial strategies. So, I finally have access to that type of person and we've already started having the type of conversations that you're talking about. I realize as the entrepreneur that we need help even in areas of pricing. We even made some mistakes there. (I chuckle a bit). So, look. I'm going to be honest with you. The financial situation that we are in right now is a blessing in disguise because it's forced us to look at things differently in terms of how we position ourselves against our competition and who we're taking advice from. So to answer your question, not only do I have someone who handles the books but I have someone far sharper than that who goes a lot further. So, I think what we need to do at this point is figure out, based on the contracts that we have right now. And look, I'm not trying to hedge my bets here. What I'm trying to do is put up a plan where I can actually pay down this loan at some affordable monthly payment. Whatever that turns out to be. Amortize it out, term it out another three years, whatever terminology you want to use. But my goal is to pay it off a lot sooner than that. Because we have paid this down before, and one thing we have done is kept the bills paid on these loans. There is no denying that. We have never missed a payment."

The Hammer: "Well, you've been fortunate in that you've been accepting interest only and we have not called the loan. (To the sales rep) You should have called the loan a year and a half ago. The total amount is due. You haven't been making ... you've been making extension payments–interest only."

Me: "But my point is I have proven that I can make the payments. I've proven that."

The Hammer: "You've proven that you've done the minimum. Okay? Nothing's wrong with that but I'm saying that you know the minimum amount that you need to do in order to keep people at bay."

Me: "Exactly. So, what I want to do at this point is I want to get beyond that. I want to focus on doing what I do best. I want to get beyond the phone calls and these meetings. Because I'm in a position right now where you probably would not have wanted to talk to me a few years ago. If I was in the position I'm in right now. But this is where we are. So, at this point I think the best thing to do is to come up with some kind of option that allows me to get this line paid down. Let's come up with some amount—"

The Hammer tries to interrupt.

Me: "Let me finish..."

The conversation goes on for several more pages and would make this chapter far too long. However, I will post the full conversation on my blog at:

www.PresidentsPilotsEntrepreneurs.com.

Things go on to get pretty heated in that room because I refused to be forced into a position of weakness and into another bad financial agreement.

Every time I listen to this exchange, I have to remind myself that I was in the room that day. Over time, The Hammer settled down and we had more meaningful discussions. This was after it became clear the usual scare tactics and mental games of chicken were not effective. I expected and demanded a good faith negotiation. This was not a show of machismo or phony bravado as fear and anxiety just did not register. Over time, I believe I gained this man's respect because I did not allow him to browbeat me. No one can force you into anything. There is always a choice even if the choices are not the most ideal. Choose to set the tone in a manner that works best for you, and do not ever fight the other guy's fight. You may not always get what you want, but you will always be respected by those across the table as well as by yourself.

In Hindsight

The direction of this hindsight should be clear. If not, reread the last few sections. When in a situation like this, a number of things can be done better. First, if you feel you must work with a bank, make a number of them compete for your business, which is what most of us do with most of our transactions. People move from store to store, car dealer to car dealer in search of the best deal. This should be no different. Second, enlist the help of a specialist in finances to help you understand minute details of the contract. Third, get the advice of successful entrepreneurs and ask them about their experiences with loan agreements. This is also an excellent group to get recommendations for banks most suitable to your situation or industry.

Again, the best advice is to avoid the banks altogether. Look for investors from among friends, family and associates if possible. This requires asking a large number of people to get enough yeses. Most of us doubt ourselves too much to pull this off. Howard Shultz sought funding for Starbucks from two hundred and forty-two individual investors. Only twenty-five of them said yes. This form of funding makes you a better entrepreneur because private investors ask tough questions, forcing you to consider issues you never thought of before. Banks want to know what they can take if you default on your loan.

The caution against banks is a general one and is not meant to imply that all banks are bad. A number of them are helpful to entrepreneurs and provide support in a number of ways. If you find this type of bank, do not be so quick to turning them away because another offers you more money. The grass is not always greener on the other side.

A bank loan is a serious responsibility not to be made light of. Once you accept the obligation, you are responsible for paying it back. The bank will not care about your lack of revenues, poor sales process or the bad weather outside. All they care about is getting their money back. The constant phone calls and emails will be a big distraction for you and your operations. Therefore, I again caution you to avoid this trap. Seek out private investors who will not only provide capital but business contacts and mentoring as well.

Key Take Aways

1. Resist seeking funding until you have a plan for its use.
2. Enlist the help of a financial advisor who has your best interests at heart to help you manage your finances. This does not include a bank.
3. The bank is not your partner. They are the lender. Maintain a pleasant relationship but do not confuse the roles.
4. Never negotiate from a position of weakness. If you feel you are in a weak position, have an advisor assist you in negotiations such as a business mentor or subject matter expert.
5. If you eventually seek out funding from a bank, make multiple banks compete for your business. Remember you are the customer, not the other way around.
6. Have an attorney review all contracts, especially financial contracts.
7. Never take the first deal offered to you. The first offer is usually just a starting point for negotiations.
8. Always understand and remember your value, despite your current situation.

7
TRUSTING YOUR GUT

I have always found that if I move with seventy-five percent or more of the facts that I usually never regret it. It's the guys who wait to have everything perfect that drive you crazy.

Lee Iacocca—

I remember watching the late Steve Jobs in a joint interview with Bill Gates. These two titans of technology together on stage were fascinating to watch. As I sat on the edge of my seat throughout the entire interview, one moment stood out more than any other. In response to a question, Jobs said the following:

"You've got to figure out how to size people up fairly quickly—make decisions without knowing people too well, and hire them and see how you do and refine your intuition."

Howard Shultz, CEO of Starbucks, put it this way in his book "Pour Your Heart Into It":

"More than most managers, I rely heavily on my instincts about people. Whether I'm hiring a key executive, selecting an investment banker, or assessing

a partner in a joint venture, I look for the same kind of qualities most look for in choosing a spouse: integrity and passion."

This is a personality trait shared by all successful entrepreneurs. From the legends portrayed on television to the local entrepreneurs I speak with on a regular basis, the uncanny ability to listen to and follow their gut is a key ingredient of their success.

Over the years my gut proved correct many times. Only when I failed to heed the signals did I end up on the wrong side of a bad decision. What this inner voice or gut feeling is, I do not know for sure, but I know it exists. Maybe future generations will identify the source like recent generations discovered radio waves. Regardless of the intricate details, the benefits of developing a healthy gut instinct are too overwhelming to ignore. The goal of this chapter is to provide tips on the use of this incredible power in your journey toward entrepreneurial greatness.

What "The Gut" Might Be

Years ago I awoke from a dream laughing hysterically and clutching my abdomen from a joke I told in the dream. As I sat on the edge of my bed unable to control the laughter, I promised myself I would write it down so I could share it with friends later. I was hungry and decided to write it down after breakfast. An hour later this hilarious gem was gone, and to this day I have no idea what caused me to laugh so hard that it brought me out of a deep sleep.

There is no doubt in my mind the clever joke is buried somewhere in my unconscious waiting to be rediscovered. I wonder if this is what the "gut" really is —some experience, encounter, thought or information buried deep in our unconscious that seeps to the surface just enough to be a whisper but not quite enough to be identified. This is why I place so much importance on the gut. It may very well be based on a piece of credible information buried too deep for us to "put our finger on it."

Learn to Trust Yourself

Knowing how and when to follow your gut boils down to trust in yourself. Lack of self trust causes us to ignore the gut and seek advice from inadequate sources. This is especially true for new entrepreneurs. In our heart of hearts we sense the right course of action but because we have not learned to trust ourselves, we seek the advice of "Uncle Joey," a person who never owned or ran a business and who can offer little in the way of guidance. For some, this is an unconscious attempt to find an excuse not to take action. Failure then becomes someone else's fault. "Well, Uncle Joey said such and such and that's what I did."

Those prone to ignore their gut find listening to the inner voice frightening. The fear sometimes propels them into a state of endless analysis but data may conflict with what the gut says. Not until they reconcile the two is a decision forthcoming. I discuss this problem in more detail later in this chapter.

The Most Effective Use of the Gut

Research by Dr. James Hayton, PhD of Newcastle University, suggests the most effective use of gut instinct is in areas we have expertise or experience. Take the case of Sam Schmidt for example. Sam was a 21-year-old involved in a five car pileup which left him in a coma. Hospital staff suggested taking him off life support because he showed no signs of recovery. Then Dr. Robert Spetzler, director of the hospital's Neurological Institute, intervened based on a hunch. He suggested staff wait one more week before putting Sam to rest. Miraculously, that very same evening Sam responded to commands. A few days later, he opened his eyes and is expected to make a full recovery.

Dr. Spetzler's gut paid off in this case in part, I believe, because of his experience in the field. Now if this doctor gave me medical advice based on his gut feeling, I may be inclined to listen. If he gave me advice on matters of financial management, also based on his gut, I would probably pass.

There is the chance, though I have no proof, that information buried deep in the doctor's mind but not fully accessible was the true source of this hunch. How many times has this same doctor advised taking patients off of life support without the aid of a hunch? Something was different about this case, which compelled the doctor to take a different course of action.

Learn to trust your gut when it comes to areas familiar to you and more times than not it will serve you well. That barely audible whisper could be the residue of past experiences or training. Although you cannot explain this in any logical fashion, the obvious benefits should not be ignored.

ANALYSIS PARALYSIS

The side effect of our fear to trust ourselves is what many refer to as paralysis by analysis. Meaning, we analyze data to such an extent, we delay making decisions. In extreme cases, decisions get made for us by our failure to act in a timely fashion. Circumstances take over and limit our choices, often in a way that are harmful. Coming from a systems engineering background, I believe strongly in the analysis of data and trends, especially in areas outside of my expertise. The purpose of data gathering is to aid the decision-making process, not to make the decision for us.

When faced with difficult decisions and those where you lack experience, thoroughly examine data collected from your experts, then "let it cook," as we used to say with regard to "burning in" newly built computers. Busy yourself with an unrelated activity, preferably something relaxing and fun, then come back later and make a decision. If at this point you are still unsure of what action to take, listen to your gut. Since you are better informed with the most relevant data available, your gut can be of better use in guiding you in the right direction. Once you make your decision, stand firm and move quickly. Do not make the mistake of second guessing or doubting yourself.

Learn to Take Small Leaps

Just because an inspiring idea hits you, does not mean you should drop everything and invest your life savings. This is what causes so many people to stop before starting—the belief that one must dive in head first with all the answers in advance when pursuing an idea. This actually works for some but not for most. Instead, take small steps to see where your mind leads you. Chances are whatever source inspired the gut feeling will reveal more of the required steps as you move along the path. This requires a great deal of faith, another common trait in successful entrepreneurs.

I experienced this while battling a difficult problem

over a period of several weeks. After deciding to put the problem aside, I got the best night of sleep I had had in weeks. The next morning I awoke with a clear action to take, something I had not considered before and that even seemed a bit strange. Not one to ignore my gut, I took a small step in the direction of my intuitions.

I went to my kitchen counter, opened my laptop and started hammering away at the problem. Even as I sat there working, seeds of doubt managed to creep in, but I continued nonetheless. The solution became clearer and clearer until it finally all made sense. Two ideas merged into one—one from several years previous and another from a few weeks earlier. If someone had suggested a similar solution, I would have called them crazy and thought nothing of the advice.

This resulted in me solving my problem and embarking on a new project I would not have thought of if left solely to conscious logic. The two separate experiences existed in my mind but my gut provided the glue for bringing them together. Had I done what most people do and wrote it off as silly, I would have missed out on a fantastic opportunity. How many product ideas and great opportunities go unrealized because of this?

The Habit of Auto Negation

What is auto negation? Okay, I admit I made up this term for lack of finding better terminology. Many people practice the destructive habit of talking themselves out of ideas almost instantly. This happens so quickly as to go unnoticed, which is how I define auto negation.

Here is a typical auto negation sequence. Some great idea flashes into your mind. You leap up in excitement at the possibilities. Then, mere seconds later you say something like, "But that's a crazy idea" or "Who would be interested in that?" You say these things as you laugh to yourself, then go back to whatever you were doing before inspiration hit. Perhaps something in your environment triggered this idea; a smell, a sound or something you touched. Something was recalled deep down inside of you which you batted away as quickly as it arrived.

The only way I know of kicking a bad habit is by deliberate effort. Nowadays I am on the lookout for this menace, and when it appears I bat it down within seconds of its arrival. The opposite of auto negation is swift action, which can be something as little as thinking through to the next steps. Whatever you do, avoid clever putdowns of yourself and move swiftly to something actionable.

Learn to Quiet The Mind

If the gut instinct is just a whisper of something deeper, then hearing a whisper in a noisy room is impossible. Noise in the form of worry, fear, anxiety and other negative emotions, keeps one from recognizing the gut when it speaks. If you suffer from self doubt, you may have missed out on a number of opportunities because you cannot risk trusting yourself. How many times have you seen some product on the market and remembered thinking of the same idea yourself? This happens to all of us at some point. The whisper came but the noise of our minds drowned out the inspiring thought.

Quieting the mind requires stepping away from your problems and focusing attention on other positive, healthy activities. Have you ever noticed how solutions to problems pop into your head while busy with something totally unrelated? This is why taking breaks throughout the day and taking vacations from time to time is so important.

Meditation in whatever form you choose is another good method because the focus is on deliberate quieting of the mind, similar to physical exercise. Call it whatever you want; prayer, meditation, zoning out. Plenty of research exists extolling the benefits of quieting the mind regularly through different forms of meditation. Muslims take regular intervals throughout the day to offer five daily prayers. Buddhists practice meditation sometimes for hours at a time. The same is true for Hindus and traditional practitioners of Yoga.

Regardless of your method, there is something to the art of deliberate quieting of the mind. With enough time and practice, the noise gets quieter, and the messages from the gut grow louder.

Do Not Fear Being Wrong

A one hundred percent rate of accuracy is impossible in anything, including following your gut. There is the chance you will misinterpret the information or fail in your execution. There is also the chance of being flat out wrong. I prefer to attempt and be wrong than to do nothing and always wonder. As you practice listening to your gut and quieting your mind, your rate of accuracy will increase, but you must first learn to trust yourself.

Seeking Advice to Aid the Gut

Remember the Gatorade "Be like Mike" commercial from back in the 80s? For those too young to remember, look up the video on the Internet. The commercial features kids on playgrounds across America imitating the moves of basketball legend Michael Jordan. So, what does this have to do with being an entrepreneur? Everything.

Do not go about seeking advice and approval from the wrong people. If you want to "be like Mike," don't ask "Uncle Joey." If you want to be successful at this game of entrepreneurship, do not seek advice from those who have no interest in entrepreneurship or who do not run a business themselves. The only exception to this rule is the advice of specialists on specific aspects of your business, such as finances. In this case, be certain the person is an expert in their field and limit the discussion to their area of expertise.

Besides these specialists, other entrepreneurs are an excellent choice. If possible, seek out entrepreneurs of a similar niche. National trade groups and associations are a great place to start. Social networking sites such as Twitter, Facebook and LinkedIn are good resources for seeking advice from those in your same niche who are not necessarily in your local area. In your local area seek out mentorships with other successful entrepreneurs. In my area, I get excellent advice from a number of successful entrepreneurs. Their advice is far more valuable than that of the "Uncle Joeys" of the world.

Be sure to use advice in the correct way and not as a way of delaying important decisions. As stated earlier, advice is a means of aiding the gut when faced with unfamiliar issues. The decision is still left to you.

In Hindsight

In my early days of entrepreneurship, I ignored my gut more times than I care to count. Tough decision-making was difficult for me at times and I sought validation from people I trusted. In the absence of the needed validation, I delayed important decisions indefinitely. One of the most memorable examples was delaying the firing of an inadequate employee. Members of my team as well as my gut said to get rid of this person but I resisted. I needed to be certain he could not be utilized elsewhere in the organization, although inside I knew better. Several months and a number of dissatisfied customers later, I finally let him go.

This delayed decision was disastrous on many levels. Not only did we lose several thousand dollars in the form of his salary and benefits, but we also lost customers. It took us over a year and many meetings to repair one of those damaged relationships. Another was irreparable and the client never did business with us again.

Another example of this failure is when I sought the advice of another entrepreneur on my decision to hire a dedicated sales person. As good as we were when in front of upper level decision makers, opening the doors and cold prospecting was a serious weakness. The entrepreneur I consulted ran a company much larger than my own, and he decided to experiment with the sales process. He was in favor of something we considered at the time—hire engineers who have the ability to sell and forego the traditional sales role.

Another entrepreneur I consulted said just the opposite. Pairing a technical salesperson with an engineer was a time tested solution that just worked. I had enough knowledge of this subject to make a sound decision. Instead, I sought advice where none was needed. All of the evidence, including my gut, pointed toward one direction, but I chose to go the opposite route. The entrepreneur with the sales experiment later dropped the idea himself and stuck with the original formula.

We must learn to trust ourselves and to value our own opinions as much as we value the opinions of others. This lack of self trust is at the heart of our inability to take action on issues when the correct course of action is clear. As the saying goes, do not allow the perfect to be the enemy of the good. Failure as a result of trying must always be preferred over the failure of inaction.

Key Take Aways

1. Do not use advice as an excuse for inaction or relinquishing responsibility. This is often done by asking advice from someone who is not in a position to be helpful.
2. Learn to trust yourself by following your gut more.
3. The gut is most effective in areas where you have expertise.
4. Seek advice from experts in specific areas of your business, but do not rely on them or the data to make decisions for you.
5. Learn to quiet the mind through different forms of meditation and giving your mind a break.
6. Take seriously hunches that seem to come from nowhere, especially those related to your areas of expertise.
7. Take small action steps when you get a gut feeling, and keep an eye on how things develop and progress.

8
TO PARTNER OR NOT TO PARTNER

A friendship founded on business is a good deal better than a business founded on friendship.
John D. Rockefeller—

Study some of the most successful companies and product launches in history, and you will find they started as teams, not individuals. Microsoft, Apple, Ben & Jerry's, Facebook, Google are a few that come to mind. There is much truth in the old saying "two heads are better than one." What is true for two, is even more so for a higher number. This type of thinking is sacrilege for many new entrepreneurs. It is also part of the reason so many fail.

Partnership in business is more a question of how, not a question of should. Though I did not always hold this view, experience has taught me that business partners who complement each other have a higher likelihood of succeeding. Entrepreneurs too often reject this idea because of an unwillingness to share profits. Would you rather have one hundred percent of something small or fifty percent of something much larger? Those who insist on operating as lone entrepreneurs, eventually end up with one hundred percent of nothing.

Put aside for now any prejudices against partnering, and read this chapter with an open mind. Partnerships executed with precision can be the difference between mediocrity and the type of success we read about in books. This chapter talks about partnering the right way and how to select the right person.

Know Thyself

Most important to consider when partnering are your own strengths and weaknesses as well as those of your business. The biggest mistake, and a common one, is to partner with someone who is similar to you. Look for someone who complements your weaknesses, not someone fun to be around because you share the same tastes.

By knowing yourself I mean really understanding what makes you tick at a much deeper level than knowing your basic passions. Do not partner with an introvert if you are an introvert yourself. If you are more of a big idea person, seek out someone with a talent for attention to details. A team full of individuals of similar types and backgrounds makes a company lopsided—strong in some areas, while extremely weak in others.

I recommend entrepreneurs gain better knowledge of themselves through personality testing along the lines of the Myers-Brigg Type Indicator or MBTI. Perform an internet search on the phrase "free mbti test." The authoritative book on this subject is by David Keirsey entitled "Please Understand Me II." Not only did I learn more about myself than ever before, but I learned to appreciate some of my personality quirks that used to annoy me. Keirsey's book also helped me understand the types of people I should surround myself with in order to maximize my strengths and shore up my weaknesses.

In addition to MBTI testing, other tests identify specific entrepreneurial types. Are you more of a specialist, a team builder or a collaborator? A specialist needs a salesperson, and a collaborator needs a specialist. The Internet has several free resources on this subject but one I find particularly interesting is EZOG, which stands for Entrepreneurial Zone of Genius. You can take the test free of charge by visiting the EZOG website at www.MyEzog.com. I took both the MBTI and EZOG tests and now have a much better understanding of my general personality type as well as my specific entrepreneurial type.

Know Thy Business

Why partner with a hotshot marketer if you have a strong marketing operation already? When considering a partner, make a list of your business' flaws, which is separate from your personal shortcomings and strengths. Then, identify the necessary qualities a potential partner must possess that will strengthen the company. This is a tough exercise because new entrepreneurs do not want to think of their businesses as flawed. Like a proud parent, we have no problem pointing out our own flaws, but cannot bring ourselves to criticize our new baby in any way. However, to ignore these steps would be foolish because you cannot manage what you cannot measure. Without identifying the soft spots in yourself and your business, you cannot create a well balanced operation.

The best way I know to do this is to take the time to write down a complete list of strengths and weaknesses in your business, including the business model itself. Be honest with yourself or else this exercise is pointless. Once complete, write down the character traits needed in a partner to help bring balance to your business. This should be a best case, sky is the limit list of characteristics. The likelihood of finding someone who meets all criteria is slim, but it gives you a checklist to score and grade future partners against. This also gives you a much clearer and more objective view of your business.

RESEARCH POTENTIAL PARTNERS

What has this person done in the past that makes them a good fit for partnership? Something even more important to consider is anything from their past that could bring harm to your business. Insist on either prior experience running a business or a unique skill that adds a competitive advantage. Perhaps your strength is in coding and your partner's in business development. Or maybe the reverse is true. Whatever the skill, it should not be the same as your own and must be substantial.

Ask for a recent tax return and a credit report. If they hesitate, send them on their way. A partner with heavy financial or tax obligations could be a burden on the company in challenging economic times. The eventual belt-tightening which accompanies all ventures will be too much for someone in such a position. This is not to say a partner must have perfect credit, but in making your decision, everything must be considered.

PUT YOUR MONEY WHERE YOUR MOUTH IS

Regardless of the partner or their unique skill, if they join an already established business, ask for a financial investment. Sweat equity or unique skills alone will not do. You want a committed partner who will be there when times get tough. The surest way to test their commitment is by asking for a cash investment. Refusal is grounds for reconsidering the partnership.

Entrepreneurs and other business professionals are all over the place on this point. Some suggest giving significant equity to talented programmers who add a competitive advantage. They argue this gives them incentive to work harder, but I still disagree. Founders who invest their own capital come to the venture with a different mindset than employees. Potential partners who do not believe enough in the venture to risk their own capital are not committed enough to stick around when times get hard. In my experience, it is difficult converting someone from an employee mindset to that of a partner or entrepreneur. An equity position does not automatically create an entrepreneur's mind. Hesitating to make a financial investment is a serious cause for concern.

GET IT IN WRITING

Whether it is your best friend, your mother or a former colleague, reduce every detail to writing. This is the job of your attorney, not Internet forums or contract templates. The attorney should draft the agreement and review the terms with all parties. This is the last chance for either party to back out or clarify any issues. Be sure to find a lawyer who specializes in business partnerships and buy/sell agreements.

Disagreements and misunderstandings are part of conducting business. Your partner agreement serves as a reminder of all clauses as well as the responsibilities of all principals. No one should object to a legal, binding agreement, nor should the process be rushed. Any party who objects to signing mutually agreed upon terms should no longer be considered for partnership.

What about dividing equity between partners? A fifty-fifty split is a bad idea for a number of reasons, chief of which being an inability to make final decisions. Someone must be the final authority in a stalemate. This is extremely difficult when partners own equal shares. If adding a partner to an already established business, there should be no quarrels with the original founder retaining a fifty-one percent or higher stake.

Why so many precautions? Besides personal experience, there is the advice of one of my mentors, whose story of a partnership gone wrong I shared in Chapter Four. He learned from his mistake and now runs a successful company with over one hundred employees. Of all the advice he ever gave me, his warnings about partnerships stand out the most. Choosing a business partner should be taken as seriously as choosing a spouse. It can be one of the best decisions if done right or one of your worst if done in a careless fashion.

In Hindsight

Now that I covered how to partner the right way, let me give you an example of how to do it the wrong way. As promised, this book is about the good, the bad and the ugly of entrepreneurship, not just the happy talk. Entrepreneurs like to keep the ugly to themselves, but I share my most difficult experiences to help those reading this book. This hindsight is the most difficult for me because I violated every rule in the book on the subject of partnering. The result was a partner who ran for the exits the moment we hit The Gauntlet.

I started one of my companies as a lone systems engineer selling services to multiple clients. As business grew, I enlisted the help of another engineer by subcontracting him as a side "gig" to his full-time job. Soon I realized the benefits of having someone to consult with on ideas. This is when I first realized the benefits of partnering and started to change my views on the subject.

A number of his qualities were ideal for my business. He was far more sociable than me and was known by people everywhere we went. It got to the point where I would joke with waitresses and ask if they knew him or if they were somehow related. Me on the other hand, I am more of an introvert who sticks primarily to work and home. To say he possessed a fantastic work ethic would be an understatement. When he threw himself into a technical problem, I knew it would get solved without me managing or overseeing his efforts. His self-managed style freed up my time and allowed me to focus attention on more important matters. To this day, I would recommend him for almost any position as an employee.

Despite his laudable qualities as a worker, I noticed a number of unsettling weaknesses that should have disqualified him as a partner. I ignored most of my concerns because clients loved his work and I billed him regularly at a substantial rate. Soon I learned a good worker does not always translate to a good business partner. He talked a lot about leaving his job and "going independent," specifically partnering in my business. Today I realize he was more enthralled with the romantic ideas of entrepreneurship and "being your own boss." His tolerance for risk was low to say the least and a steady, large paycheck was an absolute necessity.

Although he was well skilled, his were no different

than my own. Instead of bringing something unique to the company, he helped with existing overflow work. In other words, there was more work than I could handle by myself but was the type of work I did myself for years. In this regard, we were virtually the same, except for one glaring difference—he was uncomfortable and ineffective conversing with top-level management types, a skill I expected and needed in a partner. This crowd made him uneasy and boy did it show.

Despite my misgivings, I took him on as a fifty-fifty partner while he kept his full-time job. As I brought on new customers and projects, he continued to help on a part-time basis. There came a time, however, when part-time was no longer enough. Our list of clients grew as well as the amount of work, and I prodded him to leave his job. The company had reached a point where both of us could live off of the earnings, while increasing our revenues with full-time, focused effort.

To leave his job, he wanted a much higher number of clients, an unrealistic threshold that I would not be able to reach alone. I was busy with sales as well as engineering projects, so he needed to make a serious commitment if there was any chance of us succeeding. After much prodding from me, he finally left his job and committed to building the business.

Times were good in the beginning and we thought it would never end. We picked up a steady stream of projects and clients, hired our first employee and enjoyed large salaries. However, missteps in The Lobby along with a downturn in our primary target market brought us crashing back to earth. In reality, we had entered the inevitable stage called The Gauntlet. Things got really tough and really scary. Those with an employee mindset begin to unravel at this point.

As much as he tried, he could not make the

transition from employee to entrepreneur. Soon after we hit The Gauntlet, he ran for the exits and back into the arms of a full-time job. He assured me he would return once business picked up, but I knew better. Not because I did not believe the sincerity of his promise, but because I knew him all too well.

I do not blame him. I blame myself. I cajoled him into taking on responsibilities he was not ready for. In my heart, I always knew if things ever got rough, he would not stick it out. But he was a fantastic worker, I enjoyed having him around and, well, two heads are better than one. However, this is only true with the correct two heads at the table.

An entire college semester of lessons can be found in the previous section, and I wrestled with how much detail to provide. As I type these very words, I feel embarrassed to reveal so much information. The purpose, however, is to help as many entrepreneurs as possible, even if it causes me embarrassment. If people can benefit from my mistakes and lessons, then I can go to my grave feeling proud of my work.

Key Take Aways

1. Partnering is not an issue of "Should you do it." It is a matter of how to do it properly.
2. Identify your personal weaknesses and those of your business when seeking out a partner. Find a partner who complements those strengths and weaknesses.
3. Take the MBTI test to better understand yourself. Do not partner with someone who is "just like you."
4. Thoroughly research partner candidates. At a minimum, require current tax, credit and

financial statements. If they hesitate to share this information, they may not be a good candidate for partnership.
5. A partner should bring significant value to the company in an area that is severely lacking.
6. Require partners to make financial investments to prove how serious they are about the venture.
7. Avoid fifty-fifty equity splits. If you started the business, be sure to retain a fifty-one percent or higher share.
8. Have a lawyer draw up the partner agreement before starting any joint work. Take this as a time to have any concerns or questions answered.

9
JUDGE BY RESULTS, NOT BY ACTIVITY

Things which matter most must never be at the mercy of things which matter least.

Goethe—

The Marines have a saying I often repeat: Lead by example and judge by results. The second part of this saying is the subject of this chapter. People have a knack for fooling themselves into thinking they are doing important work. Then when the time comes to evaluate the results, they list a host of reasons why they did not reach their goals. Upon closer and more honest examination, the real problem becomes evident —they were simply busy being busy.

To the untrained eye this person seems like a real go-getter, while in reality they do nothing more than put on a good show. There is the lengthy task list they attack every day; the "strategy" meetings with "strategic" partners; the list of prospects that must be perfectly organized before making phone calls. They also happily take on the tasks of others because this adds to the illusion of doing important work.

The first signs of the problem appear in The Gauntlet. Apprehensive about the landscape, the nervous entrepreneur busies him or herself with the mundane, unsure of what else to do. The minute you recognize this behavior in yourself, take immediate corrective action. To judge the effectiveness of your activities, take a close look at the results. If the desired results are wanting, something is missing from your work.

GOALS VS. MILESTONES

A surefire way of falling victim to busy work, is failing to articulate your goals. Worse yet is mistaking a milestone for a goal and stopping short of the finish line. A goal is a desired end, while a milestone is a marker on the pathway to that end. Milestones let us know when we are headed in the right direction—a means of course correction along the way. If we mistake milestones for goals, we risk stopping at the milestone and falling short of our stated goals.

We made this mistake when introducing a new service. I told the sales team they needed so many meetings and product demos per week to spread the word about the new service. Well, they did exactly as instructed. Over the next few months, we had several meetings and demos, but not a single sale. They spread the word but never asked for a deal.

The following illustrates the difference between milestones and goals. Target X number of meetings (milestone) to get X number of demos (milestone) to close Y number of sales (goal). The sales team missed the Y of the equation because I never explained it. Part of the responsibility of an entrepreneur is defining the goals and direction of the business. People will not always "just get it." Do not assume or take anything for granted.

Check Your Markers Often

Just as in life, in business you must make sure your actions line up with your end goals. Every meeting, every task, every phone call must get you closer to your desired result. Simply ask yourself if the current action gets you closer or farther away. If it gets you closer, continue. If not, toss it without ceremony or remorse.

Apply the same criteria to your partners and employees. If they get off course, correct them immediately. Allowing "busy work" to go unchecked because you do not want to hurt someone's feelings is irresponsible. If the person in question continues this bad habit, either they do not understand or are unwilling to follow instructions. Either way, you have an important decision to make.

I recall an incident where a team member and I had a disagreement over priorities. He fell victim to this problem by obsessing over insignificant aspects of one of our products. Here we were with sales in the tank and difficulty paying bills, yet he sat in the office for days working on a "problem" that did not exist. Sales were the real issue, or dare I say, his lack thereof. The stress of our situation had gotten to him and he needed something to make himself feel more useful. I finally stood up and told him no one cared about this "problem" he invented. I then made it clear that he had bigger fish to fry if he planned on getting paid.

Judging Activity

An effective way of judging yourself is by checking your comfort level. If you do not feel some level of discomfort, you are not doing enough. I mean the type of discomfort you feel by doing something you fear but you know is the right thing to do, like calling the customer who you have been avoiding for days because you fear being told no.

Pick up the phone and do it now. This is more important than finishing this chapter.

If this customer is going to say no, best to get it out of the way and move on to other, more productive tasks. Then again, perhaps a yes awaits you on the other end. Either way, the time to take action is today, not tomorrow or next week. Many lost opportunities result from someone being afraid to pick up a phone.

An excellent technique is to start your day with the tasks you dread the most. This accomplishes two important things. First, the rest of your day seems easier by comparison. Second, you form the habit of tackling and completing your most important items before the day's end. As you do this consistently, positive results will follow.

I went through something similar recently. Two prospects gave the old "talk to us in the new year" routine. January came and there I sat in my office staring at the phone thinking about these two customers. Not willing to hear the dreaded "no," I moved on to other tasks. Then, I snapped out of it and decided to take a simple action–I sent a brief follow up email to inquire about the status. To my surprise, they both replied within a day to inform me they were starting the contracting process. A couple of weeks later, two new contracts were sitting on my desk.

In Hindsight

Once I had a junior salesperson who I knew had this problem, yet I let it go on far too long. This salesperson set a "goal" of making a certain number of phone calls instead of contacts. He defined a phone call as a voicemail, an unanswered line or even a wrong number. A contact, on the other hand, is talking to an actual prospect.

We defined our market as X and instructed everyone to avoid market Y. The forecast for the Y market was bleak, while we found the X market to be fertile ground. The salesperson insisted on working within his comfort zone of market Y and months later he had zero sales and very few prospects. Despite making some effort toward the more fertile market, he always gravitated back to the dying segment.

I let this destructive behavior go on longer than necessary because I wanted this person to succeed. Unfortunately, sometimes the only solution is to part ways. Failure to take corrective action in a timely manner could be the difference between making it to the Players Lounge and dying in the Gauntlet. If an employee is unable to correct their behavior, the only solution is to fire them the moment this becomes obvious.

Key Take Aways

1. Busy work is pointless, mundane tasks that fill time but do not get you closer to your goal.
2. Understand the difference between a goal and a milestone. A goal defines a definite desired result such as closing a sale. A milestone is a marker along the pathway to a goal, such as meeting with a prospective client. Check your markers often.
3. Define goals clearly and share this information with your team.
4. Take immediate corrective action against busy work.

5. Those who are unable or unwilling to correct this habit, fire them.
6. Start your day with your most difficult tasks. They may be the most important.
7. Check every task, every meeting, and every interaction against your goals. Anything that does not move you closer to your goal should be dismissed immediately.

10
SHOW ME YOUR FRIENDS

Keep away from people who try to belittle your ambitions. Small people always do that, but the really great make you feel that you, too, can become great.
Mark Twain—

"Show me your friends and I will tell you who you are," as the saying goes. I touched on the topic of right association throughout various places of this book, but such an important topic requires a more in-depth discussion. As much as we hate to admit it, those with whom we keep company have a tremendous amount of influence over us, both positive and negative. Think of anyone in your life who moved to a different region of the country or the world. Did you notice how they adopted many of the mannerisms and habits of the region, right down to the local accent in some cases? Choosing the right type of friends and associates is important in life in general, but could be the difference between success and failure as an entrepreneur.

I have friends who I love dearly and who I wish the greatest of success, but I limit my time with them because they carry in their hearts a treacherous disease. The lack of obvious symptoms makes it far worse than diseases we normally fear. People with the flu for example, suffer from coughing, runny nose, fatigue and the chills. These signs warn us to keep our distance until they rid themselves of this menace. The other more sinister disease I speak of infects the toxic personalities in our lives–those who find fault with everything and bite off their fingers with envy when others succeed. Call it cynicism, pessimism or defeatism—like cat burglars, its carriers rob us of our spirit while we lie practically unconscious.

SIGNS OF A TOXIC PERSONALITY

Toxic personalities carry a victim mentality and are miserable inside. Although they pretend to be happy for your success, their true nature eventually gives way to pretense. They hate to see others excel while they are left to waddle in the gutter, of course at no fault of their own. They veil their toxicity with clever, snide remarks that in time grow into outright hostility.

The ability to recognize toxic personality traits is invaluable in all situations but especially in entrepreneurship. The following is not a complete list but represents some of the most common characteristics.

- Always finding fault with others
- Interprets information in the most negative way
- Speaks ill of people who are not present
- Constant complaining about finances, relationships or other personal issues
- Clever putdowns disguised as jokes
- Always trying to outdo or compete with you
- Being in their company makes you feel drained
- Sheer envy

If you are lucky, they will find someone else to latch on to as your ambitions propel you to heights far out of their reach. Life is rampant with examples of friends who grow apart because one chooses to live in mediocrity, while the other sets and achieves their goals. At the least, limit your contact with these types whether they are family, friends or other associates. If possible, cut them off completely before their dark world begins to penetrate your own.

What If Your Customer is Toxic?

I recall a consulting project where many of those who worked for the customer were these exact types. They constantly complained about the most insignificant matters. No issue was too small to warrant an hour-long rant about the inherent inequities of life. Not only were problems a problem but solutions were even bigger problems. This led them to do just enough to keep upper management oblivious to their ineptness.

Not only did they carry dark clouds inside of their heads, but even managed to manifest them physically! Their area of the office was noticeably darker because they turned off the lights every morning. Some days it was like working in a cold, dark cave. The organization later moved to a newer, remodeled building with automated lighting and no light switches. These employees craved their darkness to such a degree that they climbed on their desks and unscrewed the light bulbs! Then, each morning we would arrive to a bright office with "fixed" light bulbs. This game of cat and mouse went on for several weeks until they finally relented and learned to "live in the light." This did, however, give them one more thing to complain about, which they were more than happy to do.

Regardless of your level of optimism or healthy mental state, toxic environments will eventually take a toll on you. Even a small impact is too much in my opinion, which is why I decided to limit my contact with this group of employees and over time scaled back my support of this customer.

YOU ARE NOT THE FIXER OF PEOPLE

This is a point of contention between my wife and I. Lisa is the most patient and compassionate person I have ever known. She has such a positive spirit and is so pleasant to be around that people of all types love to be in her company. She also believes toxic people can benefit by being in the presence of those who are more optimistic. On this final point is where we part ways.

Your job as an entrepreneur is to grow an enterprise, whether large or small. Unless you plan on opening a business that focuses on psychotherapy or you have a cure for chronic pessimism, you have no business attempting to "fix" the toxic people in your life. Even if you wanted to, you do not have the training to do so. Therefore, I implore you to distance yourself from these types of people as much as possible, not only in your business dealings but in your personal life as well.

EMBRACE BEING ALONE

Better to be alone than in the company of scoundrels. As I mentioned in the introduction, entrepreneurship can be a lonely existence. As you purge your surroundings of negative influences and toxic personalities, you may look up one day and find there are not a lot of people left. In time, you will fill those empty spaces with like-minded, optimistic types.

You will find them and they will find you. Today I have friends all over the world, success-oriented entrepreneurs with big ideas.

Being alone and being lonely is not the same thing. A person can be alone without experiencing loneliness. Some of the best times I have are those spent pecking away at a keyboard, reading a book or planning a big project. Hours feel like minutes and loneliness never comes to mind.

Effective Networking

By now, the types of personalities you elect to spend your time with should be obvious. They include those who have a level of success similar to or greater than what you seek for yourself. One of the best ways to connect with the right kinds of people is through networking, but like other aspects of your business, plan your networking activities with specific goals in mind. What type of people do you want to interact with and why? Are they customers, potential mentors or vendors? Plan your interactions and event participation based on the answers to these questions.

Professionals do not attend networking events just to socialize and make friends and neither should you. However, you do not want to be that guy, the one everyone recognizes and avoids. He canvasses the room handing out business cards to everyone in sight, regardless of who they are or what they do. He dominates conversations talking about himself, his business and his products, giving little consideration for the needs or wants of his audience.

Instead, walk around the room and engage in casual conversation, but do not start by reaching for a business card. If in the course of conversation there seems to be a fit and mutual interest, then is the time to exchange cards. Everyone is there to network and it is inevitable that business will come up, but most of them probably came from straight from work. They want to relax and unwind a bit, so let them. Leaping at everyone in the room with your business card reeks of desperation and inexperience.

The same rules apply to social networking as with traditional networking. Imagine walking into a room full of people and everyone rushes to you in an attempt to sell something. What would you think of them? Well, this is no different than those who bombard our Twitter feeds with the latest deals on dog food. What if I do not own a dog!?

Someone on Twitter recently tweeted me a direct message regarding their weight loss products. There are pictures of me on Twitter, the blog for this book and on Facebook and I clearly am not in need of a weight loss program. I am usually pretty cordial on Twitter but this one just annoyed me. So, I messaged the person back and said, "If you took the time to read my profile, you would know I do not need your product."

Show respect for the people in your social networking circles by first getting to know them. Read their profiles and visit their websites in search of something interesting that makes you want to engage them. Interactions will then come across as more genuine and sincere because the discussion will center on mutual interests. Offer tips, advice, blogs and articles you think could be helpful, which include articles from your own blog site as well. Just be sure to mix it up, and do not pretend to have all the answers. At the appropriate time offer them your product or service and explain why you think it is beneficial to them. Do not attempt to "sell" where no real need exists. I cover this more in Chapter Eleven.

A Divided House

What do you do when the toxic personality is your spouse? What if you cannot get them to see things your way? Unfortunately, there is no easy answer except to say the following: We all get one shot at this thing called life. At some point, we must decide to live our lives for ourselves or for others. Those who choose the latter often reach old age full of regrets and what ifs.

In my early twenties, I met an extremely wealthy gentleman who told me of the time his wife talked him out of a business investment. One day he came home excited about a franchise opportunity of which he could be one of the earliest franchisees. He pleaded for her support but she would not budge. This new franchise is what we know today as McDonald's. Years later he came home with another idea which she again tried to talk him out of. She relented when he reminded her of the last time he took her business advice. He went on to start several businesses and became a very wealthy man.

Do all you can to gain your spouse's support before starting a business. Not having this support is difficult in ways I cannot fully describe. Disclose all of your plans and address any objections or concerns up front. If they have good ideas, explore them, and involve them in areas where they can be helpful. You may find their input useful. However, I do caution against involving a reluctant spouse too much. Their involvement could undermine progress during times of stress, even if unintentional. Ultimately, you need to decide if your relationship is sufficiently strong enough to withstand the risks and stress of running a business.

In Hindsight

Let us go back to the customer with the toxic employees. I made the mistake of thinking my ironclad optimistic nature could not be affected by a group of grouches, but I was wrong. The project went from a limited engagement to an extended one of me living in a cubicle for five days a week. Then I noticed something disturbing that I shared with my wife. I slipped into a state of complacency and felt generally less energetic. This also negatively affected the quality of my work. I found myself becoming more pessimistic and joining in on the "inequities of the world" discussions. Like a bolt of lightning, I suddenly realized I was stuck in a trap of my own making.

Once I recognized the problem, I took immediate action. I thoroughly assessed my work and determined the "project" was no longer a project at all. It had transitioned into a staff augmentation position, similar to that of an employee. I decided to scale back my time with this customer and focused my efforts on other customers and projects. Over time I went from five days a week to three days a week to two days a week and to eventually ending the project.

What was most alarming about this situation is that many of the toxic people were not actual employees. They were full-time augmented "consultants" who themselves fell into a state of complacency. I made the conscious decision not to become one of them and transitioned out as quickly as I could. A couple of years later, most of them were let go.

Key Take Aways

1. Purge your personal and business environment of toxic personalities.
2. It is not your job to fix toxic people or to make them more optimistic.
3. Plan your networking activities around your primary goals and objectives.
4. Seek to build relationships and make personal connections when attending networking events or joining social networking sites.
5. Work to get your significant other on board with your entrepreneurial plans before launching. Listen to their objectives and address them. Involve them where possible.
6. Get used to being alone. This is preferred to being surrounded by toxic personalities.
7. Even customer environments can be toxic.

11
SERVING THE CUSTOMER

I never perfected an invention that I did not think about in terms of the service it might give others. I find out what the world needs, then I proceed to invent.
Thomas Edison—

Without customers, entrepreneurs are doomed, no matter the amount of investment capital or breakthrough products. Customers are inundated with emails, phone calls and mailings expounding the qualities of such and such widget. Businesses are so busy selling, they forget about servicing their customers. In response, customers have become cynical and suspicious of salespeople and entrepreneurs. It is therefore imperative entrepreneurs focus on making their services and products superior and unique. Not only is this possible, but possible with just about any product.

The entrepreneurs who stand out do more than sell. They find a way to inject their personal passions into their businesses, regardless of the products or services offered. In today's fast-paced world of "always be selling," those who slow down to listen and add real value earn the right to ask the customer for their business.

What Competition?

Everyone talks about the importance of knowing your competition in order to best position products and services. In my experience, before focusing on the competition, you must first focus on yourself. What makes you different and unique from other individuals? What is it about you that draws praise from others—the distinguishing characteristics that make you stand out? People naturally excel at things they are passionate about, but do not always see how those passions fit into their work. To make competition irrelevant, identify these traits and integrate them with your products and services. In my case, it is my writing and speaking abilities.

Writing and public speaking are two of my passions but how do you integrate them into a technology company? This was an easy question when I started a technology consulting company in 2000. Systems engineers and techies are terrible at documenting their work, which customers find extremely frustrating. This was a regular complaint from management. Something else that was not an issue until I made it one was off-site training; technical staff attending training sessions away from the job while work and system issues piled up.

I made comprehensive system documentation and onsite training my competitive advantage. While most companies parachuted in, installed systems, and then left in a rush, I took my time to carefully document my work and hold customized training sessions for customer staff. My sessions included printed training materials developed specifically for the customer.

One such example was the customer I talked about in Chapter Two, who gave me my first contract. Upon completion of the project, I handed over a one hundred and twenty-page bound document, something done by only much larger companies. This customer worked with several large and small companies over the years, but said they never received such thorough documentation. I went on to complete a number of lucrative projects with them, in large part due to my documentation and training services.

A number of companies provided similar technology services as my own, but I turned my passion for writing and public speaking into competitive advantages. I was confident other technical companies could not compete with me in these areas. In meetings with prospective clients, I emphasized these services and gave samples of documentation. With this approach, you can distinguish yourself from so-called competition, even in a crowded field.

Is a Doctor a Salesperson?

Ever complain about your doctor trying to sell you something? Probably not, because doctors do not attempt to sell us anything—their job is to help us solve problems. However, a doctor's office is a business where we pay them for their services. The difference is that we believe doctors genuinely want to help us, which often is the case. All businesses would have far more business than they could manage if they learned to deal with customers in a similar fashion.

Think of your customers as patients visiting your medical practice, and listen closely to diagnose their problems. Your customers are people and they want to be heard. How can you claim to have the perfect solution to their problem when you do not fully understand what the problem is? A doctor can make a sound diagnosis only by asking enough of the right types of questions. Otherwise, they risk prescribing the wrong medication and harming the patient. You risk the same by spending all of your time highlighting product features that are irrelevant to your customer.

We had a meeting with a customer who had spent a year worrying about a technology upgrade. At the time we met them they had a number of proposals from local companies who did not take the time to sit down with them. These companies heard of the upcoming upgrade and sent unsolicited, cookie-cutter proposals. We learned of the project through another department in the same company and the technology in question was one of our specialties. The department head passed on our contact information to upper management who invited us in for a meeting.

By the time we met, the project manager for the group was in no mood to talk. It was obvious she was there against her will and preferred to be elsewhere. She let us know she was tired of companies sending proposals with little consideration for the uniqueness of her computer network. She then crossed her arms and looked right through me.

For the next twenty minutes I asked a multitude of questions because I found their challenges very intriguing. Each of their answers provoked more questions until the complex nature of their problems became clear in my mind. Then, just to be sure, I relayed my understanding of their problems in the form of more questions. Before long, the once reluctant project manager began frantically taking notes. About fifty minutes into the meeting, she asked how soon we could get them a proposal. A few weeks later we began working on their one hundred thousand dollar upgrade project.

Your customers will tell you how to win their business if you close your mouth and open your ears. Imagine walking into a doctor's office and being handed a prescription before having the opportunity to explain your illness. As ridiculous as this sounds, it is what most people do when attempting to offer products and services.

DON'T JUST DELIVER, OVER DELIVER

When a customer accepts your proposal and grants you a contract, you have won the right to serve. Not only is this the time to deliver on your promise, but time to over deliver. Anything less than over delivery is mediocre in my opinion. Few things in life are more frustrating than someone who over promises and under delivers. This happens so often in the world of business that customers have come to expect it. Ever had a customer who was hostile and suspicious? This is the reason.

To create a loyal, repeat customer make a deliberate attempt to deliver more than you promised. In a world where sub-par service is the norm, you can stand out in a crowded field by delivering just a little extra. This does not require you giving away thousands of dollars in free service or products. For example, on a recent project we learned the customer started another project in an area where we have a great deal of expertise. Restricted budgets forced them to keep the project in-house but they lacked the expertise and were learning on their own. The customer mentioned this in passing in a status meeting, so I offered to give advice and assistance if needed. Then I went a step further by loaning them one of the best books on the subject. I told them to keep the reference as long as they wanted and to simply follow the author's guidance. This did not cost me anything but went a long way in winning the loyalty of this customer.

Accept That You Cannot Help Everyone

By pure accident, I stumbled on something that yields sales where none existed previously. There seems to be something magical about this phrase because most of the time it results in the customer saying something like, "Well, wait a minute. Maybe we do have some work for you." What is my magical set of words? "Sounds like I cannot help you but maybe we can find an opportunity to work together in the future."

Before meeting with a potential customer, I accept that there is a chance I do not have a product or service that can help them. If I discover in the course of a meeting that my services will not benefit the customer, I simply say so. No high-pressure sales or forcing products down their throats. I close up my portfolio and prepare to leave. What I learned by accident is how much customers appreciate this approach because it removes the pressure of a sales meeting. They no longer feel like they are being sold but rather being heard.

I experienced this recently when a customer stopped me as I stood up from the meeting table. A service I mentioned earlier in the meeting re-entered the conversation. The Chief Information Officer decided the service would indeed be beneficial and asked us to send a statement of work. A few weeks later, this became a fifteen thousand dollar sale.

Now I start all of my sales meetings by letting the customer know I may not have the solution to their problem. This relieves the pressure and encourages a more open discussion instead of them expecting to be sold. If by the end of the meeting I have nothing to offer, I keep my promise and leave. This is such an unusual experience in today's world of high sales quotas and quarterly earnings that there is a very good chance of hearing from this customer later and striking a deal. However, the key is sincerity. Customers are forgiving of a lot of things. Fake sincerity is not one of them.

No, the Customer is not Always Right

Despite this oft-repeated beautiful cliché, the customer is not always right. Anyone in business for any length of time knows this cliché is far from reality. Beneath this beautiful phrase, however, is a message not fully embraced by enough businesses today—we should serve our customers in the way we wish to be served ourselves.

However, what do you do when you honestly provide the best service possible and the customer is unreasonable or difficult? An entrepreneur complained to me recently of how a customer "forced" her to take a low rate. Another complained of an abusive contract they were "forced" into that nearly sunk the company. In each conversation, the word "forced" stood out like a pile of charcoal in a field of snow. Around the same time, another local company made news by rejecting the terms of a large government contract bid. By rejecting the terms, this company was disqualified from bidding on this multi-million dollar opportunity. While everyone thought the company was crazy for not agreeing to the terms, they pushed back on the local government and successfully had the contract pulled. Reportedly, a new bid is in the works with more favorable terms for all the bidders.

All of the above experiences can be reduced to one word, a word that is the overarching theme of this book:

Value. The third company understood its value and refused to allow anyone to force them into an unfavorable agreement. No one can force you into anything. The choice to enter a bad deal is all your own. Any customer who insists on making unreasonable requests—and it is up to you to define what is unreasonable—does not deserve to benefit from your service. That is, if you provide the type of service I described earlier in this chapter. If a deal does not feel right, it probably is not.

In Hindsight

Like so many growing companies, we lost focus on the qualities that made us stand out in the first place. The same company that offered me my first opportunity back in the early 2000s was very disappointed in my service years later. Not that the service was sub-par, but it was not my personal best and they knew it. Instead of delivering the same type of stellar documentation they had grown used to, I gave them a PDF file lacking detail. Was it still better than most of the competition? It sure was, but once you give someone the best, good is no longer good enough.

This customer's loss was the gain of others, for we gave new customers the red carpet treatment from start to finish. The advice in this chapter was followed to the letter, which is what made us successful. However, it is common knowledge that selling to existing customers is easier and far cheaper than acquiring new ones. The existing customer already bought from you and trusts you. Even if you do not have something new to sell, you may be surprised when you pick up the phone to call.

One such experience happened with a customer who had not bought service from us in several months. I decided to send them an email one day as a joke and to get a meeting for the following week. Here is the email I sent:

"Hello, Anne. I just wanted to inform you that I will be remoting into your network to do a massive upgrade. Don't worry. I will do a fantastic job, but understand I will also send you a bill. Ready or not, here I come. Ha ha."

Here's Anne's reply, which came a couple of days later:

"We're ready! Well, not really but we have to do this now. We have a lot that needs to be fixed. Can you come in next week."

This discussion resulted in what is called an open purchase order. In layman's terms this means fix the problem regardless of the cost. Once we fixed the problem, the customer granted us another large upgrade project. The combined projects lasted more than eighteen months. All of this because of an email I sent that was meant as a joke.

I reached out to them at a time they were experiencing pain. Previous successful projects were enough to convince them of my ability to complete the job. How many of your own customers are experiencing pain right now? When is the last time you reached out to them? Do yourself a favor and do the following the moment you complete this chapter.

1. Make a list of everyone who ever bought from you.
2. Determine any new products or services that may be beneficial to those customers.
3. Pull out your calendar and set one to two hours on the next business day to call each of them.

4. Make this procedure part of your normal routine by creating a recurring task in your calendar.

The above steps will go a long way in turning things around in your business. You may even end the day with a new contract. A great deal of effort and care goes into building strong customer relationships. A relationship that takes years to build can be undone by a single careless act. Remember to treat each customer as if they were your only customer, and they will reward you with repeat business for many years to come.

KEY TAKE AWAYS

1. Find a way to integrate your passions into your products and services.
2. Listen to your customers the way you expect a doctor to listen to you. Do not prescribe before being sure you understand the problem.
3. Lookout for opportunities to deliver extra value. Every delivery should go beyond what you promised.
4. Start new customer meetings by honestly letting them know you may not be able to help them. If your product or service is not a fit for them, keep your promise and leave without pressuring them.
5. Do not allow yourself to be forced into a bad deal. If it does not feel right, it probably isn't.
6. Never deliver less service than in previous engagements with a customer. If you do, it will be noticed even if your service remains superior to your competition.
7. Create a list of all previous customers and set

a recurring schedule to call them to introduce new services and products as well as to learn about their current challenges.

12
EMBRACING FAILURE

Most great people have attained their greatest success just one step beyond their greatest failure.
Napoleon Hill—

What does it mean to "embrace" a thing? The dictionary meaning is to "hold closely in one's arms, especially as a sign of affection." Another is to "accept or support willingly and enthusiastically." Failure is a part of entrepreneurship that all entrepreneurs eventually experience whether they like it or not. Most people have an unrealistic fear of failure that keeps them in a perpetual state of mediocrity, doing just enough to prevent total failure, but not quite enough to realize their greatest ambitions. Entrepreneurs who fall into this trap risk permanent (psychological) failure, of never attempting again. They resign to a "safe" existence, convincing themselves that cubicle life as an employee is not so bad after all.

So What If You Fail

Ask yourself, if you fail, how long would it take to get back on your feet and recover your losses? Entrepreneurship is a series of failures followed by a string of breakthroughs. The number and degree of failures depends on whether you are a fast or slow learner. Fast learners get through the failures and learn the necessary lessons quickly, then move on to the breakthroughs. Slow learners must go through many failures and extended periods of hardship before they finally get the message. The faster you gain the education that accompanies failure, the better. Therefore, instead of avoiding or fearing failure, entrepreneurs should welcome it as an able instructor.

You don't have to tell yourself, "I know I'm going to fail." That sort of defeatism has no place in entrepreneurship and will likely result in the worst type of failure—the type that prevents a person from making a sincere effort. The point is to get out of your comfort zone and expect difficulties along the way, applying the lessons learned as you move along your path. This is the true meaning of embracing failure and difficulty.

Remember It is all a Game

I went through Marine Corps boot camp many years ago and it was one of the most stressful periods of my life. One cannot appreciate the life of a Marine recruit without having lived through it. However, the first half of the movie "Full Metal Jacket" did a pretty good job of capturing the essence of the experience. For ninety days you live in isolation while some intimidating characters scream colorful epithets in your face and describe in graphic detail what they would like to do to your mother, your sister, your girlfriend and just about every female close to you. I cannot begin to count the amount of failures experienced by recruits before being granted the coveted title of "The Few, The Proud."

The job of the ever-intimidating Drill Instructor or DI is to orchestrate dozens of failures over a ninety-day period so recruits can absorb the lessons necessary to become faithful Marines. In the midst of the humiliation, confusion and sheer terror, it was hard for me to appreciate the methods of the DIs. Then, about a year after graduating boot camp, I experienced something I will never forget. I visited my old recruit depot in San Diego, California and witnessed DIs absolutely terrorizing young recruits on the parade deck. The parade deck resembles a massive parking lot and is where scores of seventeen and eighteen-year-olds first learn how to march in step. As one of the DIs passed by me screaming at the top of his lungs at his recruits, he turned to me with a bright warm smile and chimed, "How's it going?" He did this only when he knew the recruits were well ahead of him where they could not witness the interaction. The DI then turned his attention back to his ragtag group of wannabe jarheads, once again screaming until his veins pulsed violently in his neck.

    I stood there mouth agape as they marched off into the distance. I knew all along this was just a game—a very serious game of course, but witnessing this first hand as an outside observer was stunning. What if I had understood this before entering boot camp, expecting the failures and embracing them along the way? I would have learned a lot more and much faster, and I could have applied the lessons in near real time.

BE YOUR OWN DRILL INSTRUCTOR

    Entrepreneurship is also a serious game, but still a game nonetheless. All games have their ebbs and flows, ups and downs, successes and failures. Embrace the failures knowing they are there to help you succeed in the long run, and understand failure is only temporary.

Throughout boot camp I regularly reminded myself of the temporary nature of the hardships. I often imagined how great I would feel when it was all over. Just knowing that it was temporary is what got me through the experience. I detail this experience at the end of the book in order to make a larger point of not accepting failure as an option. This experience changed my life forever.

As an entrepreneur, you do not have a DI to force you out of your comfort zone. You are the DI, minus the putdowns and imaginative descriptions of your mother. Expect failure, embrace it, learn from it and apply the lessons in real time along the way. Entrepreneurs who jump in expecting immediate success set themselves up for devastating disappointments. Those who anticipate failure, while knowing it is only temporary, stand a much better chance of succeeding in a big way.

THROWING IN THE TOWEL

Like so many other clichés, "winners never quit, and quitters never win" sounds good on paper but is far from reality. In the game of entrepreneurship, winners quit often but what they do after quitting is what distinguishes them from the rest of society. To quit is one thing. To lose hope and never attempt again is quite another matter.

Successful entrepreneurs tend to retool and reinvent themselves, as opposed to all out quitting. If an idea proves unworkable, they may tweak it around the edges or chuck it altogether. Then move on to try something different. Others may hang on until the bitter end until they eventually go broke. Although defeated, they still remain optimistic and seek out other opportunities. In the case of entrepreneurship, winners never quitting is to never give up hope of being successful despite setbacks, temporary defeats and failures.

There are a number of famous examples of entrepreneurs who gave up on one idea but went on to make breakthroughs in related businesses. Bill Gates' first software company was not Microsoft. It was Traf-O-Data, which made only a few thousand dollars in revenue. Gates, along with his co-founders Paul Allen and Paul Gilbert, designed the Traf-O-Data system to read data from traffic counters, the small black rubber hoses we occasionally drive over. A number of circumstances forced the company to shut down, including the government deciding to offer similar services free of charge. Instead of hanging on until the bitter end and blaming their woes on the government, Gates and Allen took the lessons learned from the experience and later launched Microsoft.

Henry Ford's first attempt at revolutionizing automobiles was not the Ford Motor Company we know today. His first company was Detroit Automobile Company, which shut down in 1901. He then made a second attempt which also failed. Were it not for private investors, his third crack at it would have failed as well and we may not have a Ford Motor Company today.

Even myself—my first attempt with a tech company was something I called PC Doc-Tours in the mid-Nineties. I made house calls (get it) to work on my customers' computers in their homes. The business was an abysmal failure, but I sure learned a lot about customer service, marketing and why I did not want to be in the PC hardware business. At that time I could not imagine a day when I would have one million dollars worth of purchase orders and projects sitting on my desk, and I certainly could not imagine authoring a book on the subject of entrepreneurship.

So, I'm not going to tell you when to quit your business. The best advice I can give is to know your limits, collect as much data as possible, consult with trusted advisors and then follow your gut. If you do decide it is time to throw in the towel, do not see it as a total failure but an opportunity to gather lessons to apply to your next venture.

In Hindsight

Throughout this book, the Hindsights have been things I could have done better but I can honestly say when it comes to the subject of business failures, I don't have many regrets. My failures have taught me too much, like the nagging teacher you hated in grade school who you later came to adore as you graduated high school. My so-called failures supplied me with the material to author this book, which you can now benefit. They aided me in creating other successful businesses, and I am confident they will assist me in ways I have not yet discovered. I have learned to embrace and appreciate so-called failures. Do yourself a favor and learn to do the same.

Key Take Aways

1. Failure is never permanent and can even be beneficial if we learn from the experience.
2. Do not fear failure. Embrace it as a necessary part of growth as an entrepreneur.
3. It is not true that "winners never quit." Never quitting means not giving up hope of being successful even while failing a number of times.
4. There are a number of examples of famous entrepreneurs who failed multiple times before attaining success.

5. Only you know when it is time to give up your venture. Gather all necessary data, seek advice from trusted advisors, and then follow your gut.
6. Do not allow failure to prevent you from attempting again.

13
STRIKING BALANCE

I believe that being successful means having a balance of success stories across the many areas of your life. You can't truly be considered successful in your business life if your home life is in shambles.
Zig Ziglar—

There is a common joke among entrepreneurs: You can set your own hours, any twelve to eighteen hours of the day you wish. The public loves courageous tales of founders sleeping under desks while living off of pizza and Coke. Stories of this type fascinate laypeople because they always end in triumphant finishes. This is what popular culture would have us believe. In reality, most end in broken bank accounts and broken relationships.

All professionals struggle with striking the right balance between work and personal life. This is even more so for entrepreneurs and oft-times feels impossible. This is where the advice of a spouse or significant other proves invaluable. When they tell you it is time for a break, listening to them is a good idea.

TAMING THE ADRENALINE BULL

Sleep seems more like a distraction than a necessity during the early days of a venture or project. We all experience moments when adrenaline, brought on by excitement and optimism, is all the fuel we need to break through barriers. I experienced this natural high while preparing the introduction and release of this book.

I publicized the Facebook fan page and uploaded the last revision of the sample content on Sunday, November 13, 2011 at 3:30 p.m. I stayed up past 3 a.m. polishing the text and making final edits. By 7 a.m., I was out of bed and at it again. Despite a lack of sleep and food, I worked throughout the day like a well-programmed cyborg. The self imposed 3:30 p.m. deadline was fast approaching, which I did not intend to miss. As my wife and kids moved about busily through the house, I hardly noticed them at all. I sat perched for hours in front of my laptop banging away on the keyboard.

Something strange happens to the human brain during these periods. With adrenaline comes superhero-like characteristics such as heightened awareness, focus, concentration, strength and energy. Entrepreneurs perhaps experience this phenomenon more often than most, along with other creative types, I imagine. But once we reach the goal and the subject of our excitement subsides, we suddenly realize the need for sleep. This is what happened to me that day. Fatigue hit me like a ton of bricks as I read the last of the congratulatory comments. I was completely spent and realized I had slept less than five hours during the previous two days.

Some of our most productive moments happen when our old friend adrenaline shows up, but we tend to notice only after it has come and gone. For best results, learn to recognize these times and ride the adrenaline bull to the finish line. When you feel that familiar rush of excitement, consciously throw yourself into your work, stopping only for occasional water and bathroom breaks. Because this is the source of your excitement and energy, do not allow anyone to interrupt you. Otherwise, your energy decreases, making it almost impossible to recapture the moment.

Even more effective but difficult to pull off, is to psyche yourself into a rush. You can achieve this by focusing intently on your project and its most exciting elements. Then, without hesitation, get right to work once the excitement builds within you. This requires a lot of imagination and a great deal of patience but once you are good at it, it is like a wonder drug.

A poor method is to put off work until the last moment, which brings on fear, anxiety and worry. This too can induce an adrenaline rush, but the physical and psychological harm associated with these negative emotions makes this an undesirable strategy.

Even now at 10:08 p.m. on December 31, 2011, as everyone else is out welcoming in the New Year, I sit here at my laptop riding a dose of adrenaline and drinking a cup of Turkish coffee—not excited about the New Year, but about this new and exciting project. My book on entrepreneurship. I have had forty-two New Year's Eves and after a while they are just about the same. So, I will not let go of this adrenaline bull before the appointed time. But I know the wall is coming, and when it does I will let things happen naturally and drop like a rock.

EVEN SUPERHEROES NEED THEIR SLEEP

Once you come down from this rush, take heed to the signals sent by your body. Go to sleep. Attempting any work beyond this point will take you from superhero to super zero. This is the realm of foolish mistakes, which is where many go wrong.

Working twelve, sixteen or eighteen-hour days is achievable and even effective when done in the right way. However, effort beyond a certain point is not only unproductive, but also counterproductive—having the opposite of the desired effect and undermining previous progress. Once your project settles down and your life returns to something resembling normalcy, get back to a regular sleep pattern. This is one of the best things you can do for a healthy mind, a healthy business and healthy relationships.

WORK THAT BODY

In a word, exercise. No need to train for the Olympics or take up activities you have no interest in. This should be relaxing and fun. Choose something enjoyable that forces the body to physical exhaustion, and then perform this activity on a regular basis. All night coding sessions do not count. Take brisk walks; do pushups in the morning; play volleyball with your neighbors. The choice of activity is not as important as making the commitment and remaining consistent.

Outdoor activities with friends are ideal because you get to exercise and socialize at the same time. This also helps to quiet the mind. Flashes of inspiration or solutions to problems may surprise you during these times. Pay close attention if this happens. Take a brief moment to document the thought or text a colleague. But do not leave your recreational activity to rush back to the lab or office. This is leisure time and is essential to your success and overall health. Oh, and no toxic friends allowed!

Remember the Community

Do not enter the game of entrepreneurship just to make money. Make your business a means to a worthwhile end. Improve the quality of life of yourself, those closest to you and your surrounding community. Do not delay your contribution to the community, waiting to first hit it big. Do whatever little you can in the place you are in today. You do not want to be remembered as the guy who died in his office coding at 3 a.m.

Right now, I have a group of young adults that I work with every Saturday. With few exceptions, my activities with these youths fill my Saturdays from the early afternoon to late in the evening. Even during times when business is dreadful, I do not give up these activities. It helps me to keep things in perspective as well as to quiet my mind. If you have similar types of community activities, do not give them up for the sake of business. If you do not have one, find one.

Vacations are a Must

A vacation done the right way can be one of the best things for your business. My wife dragged me on a California vacation a couple of years ago, even though I resisted up until the last moment. I was convinced the company needed me when in reality, things were going quite well and I could afford to get away. We settled on a compromise of me returning home a few days ahead of her and the kids. This was one of the smartest things we ever did. I returned to work with a new vigor and freshness that lasted for weeks. It also allowed me to spend some much needed alone time with the love of my life.

We left the kids with her mom and sisters, while we took off to a beach resort for two full days of relaxation. A photo of me sitting on the beach taking in a golden sunset serves as a time machine returning me to that very moment. The melodious tune of waves lightly sweeping the coastline and the fresh smell of the Pacific Ocean to this day places me in a state of tranquility. Imagine how it felt actually being there.

A vacation does not have to be expensive or elaborate. Stay overnight with friends, family or at a hotel. Take a day trip to a nearby town. The point is to change environments. Some of the best ideas surface during these moments of rest.

Let's Talk About Sex

I will not delve too deep into this topic other than to remind you that sex is one of the best relievers of stress there is. Here I refer to loving, meaningful sex with your spouse, not anything on two legs in a smoky nightclub. Like all the other suggestions in this chapter, this activity also helps keep things in perspective.

Some Final Thoughts

Most of what is in this book can be summarized in one word: Value. In order to succeed at the game of life and the game of entrepreneurship, you must place a high degree of value on yourself. We are not defined by credit scores, revenue reports or by perceived success or failure. We are defined by what we determine is important for us.

For me, entrepreneurship is a means to an end, not an end in and of itself. The end goal is to provide a better quality of life for my family, my community and everyone I meet. If we sincerely commit ourselves to the service of others, success will follow naturally. Those who provide the best service reap the best rewards.

I hope I served you well with this work. I shared flaws, mistakes and other information we entrepreneurs prefer to keep to ourselves. I also shared successes and triumphs, which we love to boast about. This was in an effort to serve you, the reader, with all I have to offer. As you can imagine, I found difficulty sharing some of my experiences, but I feel it is my duty to help those who choose to travel this path.

Whether you are an entrepreneur, the family member of someone, or a guy who just digs the title, I wish you all the happiness and satisfaction this world has to offer. But just remember, happiness and satisfaction are products of what is inside, not outside. Godspeed and I look forward to seeing you in the Players Lounge.

KEY TAKE AWAYS

1. Learn to use the excitement of adrenaline by recognizing it and working through it without interruption.
2. Remember to return to a regular sleep pattern once the excitement of the adrenaline rush subsides.
3. Do not attempt to work beyond the adrenaline wall as it will be the source of costly mistakes and errors.
4. Find regular community activities unrelated to work to help balance out your life.
5. Take regular vacations to recharge, even if just for a couple of days in a neighboring town. The point is to remove yourself from your current environment.
6. Do not neglect regular sex with your spouse–loving, meaningful sex. The more often, the better.

Epilogue

WHAT IF FAILURE WERE IMPOSSIBLE?

Twenty years from now you will be more disappointed by the things that you didn't do than by the ones you did do.
Mark Twain—

I read a fantastic book recently by Dorothea Brande entitled "Wake Up and Live." This little book was first published back in 1936 and is barely 100 pages. Dorothea Brande makes a profound statement in this book that completely changed her life when she reached this realization - "Act as if it were impossible to fail." She goes on to state:

"Always your first question to yourself should be, What would I be doing now if it were really impossible for me to fail..."

Many will find this to be a difficult statement. How does one pretend that failure is impossible? This is the wrong question, for it is not a matter of pretending or psyching oneself out. It is a matter of belief, which all of us have experienced at some point in our lives if we would only go digging in our memory banks. Think of a time when you believed you *had* to succeed because the stakes were so high. The following are two personal examples that changed my life forever.

SHE LOVES ME NOT

My kids love this story, I think because it humanizes their parents a lot more and has a spark of storybook romance. This is one of those rare examples where truth is stranger than fiction. This is the story of when I decided to marry my wife. Before you assume this subject has nothing to do with entrepreneurship or overcoming failure, continue reading.

I remember the first time we met. I walked into the office at MAG-39, Camp Pendleton, CA to drop off some documents and up walks to the counter this little Latin cutie who refused to laugh at any of my jokes. I thought to myself as I left, *what's her problem*? Long after we had been married, she told me exactly what her problem was that day. In her eyes, she saw nothing but another cocky Marine with a loud, filthy mouth. She had not even seen the worst as I had just returned from Desert Storm and was going through my "wild streak". This makes our eventual matrimony all the more miraculous.

Several weeks later, after seeing her a number of times moving about the barracks, I decided to ask her out. This, despite one of my best friends insisting she would never have me. I was told Escobar would not give me the time of day—that she seemed to prefer a different type and I need not bother trying. Had I hesitated to consider the advice, I would have lost my nerve. How many times did you allow someone to talk you out of something important at the very moment you readied yourself for action?

I returned to my office and headed straight to the phone without sitting down. When she picked up, I somehow mixed up our names and said something like, "Hey Jones, this is Escobar. I wanted to see if you'd like to go out this weekend. Wait, I mean—." She laughed a bit as I corrected myself but to my surprise she agreed without hesitation. She even sounded happy that I called.

I remember only two things from the date. First, she ordered one of the most expensive meals on the menu—steak and shrimp. I stared at her in disbelief while she placed the order but of course, I would have been crazy to protest. I did, however, make a mental note to take her to Burger King next time.

The second thing I remember is what change everything and is the point of this entire story. After dinner we went to a dance club in San Diego but spent most of our time sitting at our table talking, both of us clearly nervous throughout the night. We had a lengthy drive back to the base, about forty minutes on interstate 5 with the glow of the moon reflecting off of the Pacific Ocean the entire way. I do not remember much from the drive except the smell of the ocean, the peacefulness of the evening and things just feeling *right*. Somehow, I found the courage to mutter those oft repeated, lame first date words: "Can I see you again some time?"

With her head resting and reclined back on her seat, she turned and look up at me with a pair of big brown eyes and smiled as she said, "Sure, but understand I am not looking for a relationship."

Why this moment had such an impact escapes me—perhaps the cadence of her soft voice or the look in her eyes. But I thought to myself right then, *I am going to marry this woman*. From that point on, the issue was settled in my mind. Of course, she did not entertain such thoughts herself, but in time that would all change. I was convinced.

The next morning I hurried out of bed and headed down to the pay phone in the barracks to call a couple of women I had seen off and on. I told them I was done with all women except for this one—officially off the market as I had found the girl of my dreams.

At no time during the course of our relationship did I entertain any other outcome but marriage. Over the next few months our relationship grew and the affections became mutual. A little over a year after our first date, we married on July 7, 1992.

From the Halls of Montezuma

This next experience began in 1988 when I enlisted in the United States Marine Corps under what is called "open contract." Open contract means a person enters the Corps without choosing a job specialty. The job is chosen instead upon completion of boot camp. I later realized a few important details were missed. Intent as I was on becoming a Marine, open contract meant almost certainly being assigned to the infantry—the grunts. The thought of becoming a Marine excited me, but imagining my next four years in "the bush" was depressing. Remember, at the time we had no "once in a generation" type wars taking place like we have today. America was at peace as the once powerful Soviet empire and communism were in rapid decline. As much respect as I had and still have for the grunts, infantry duty simply did not interest me. Therefore, I needed to find a solution for the corner I had painted myself into.

There was only one way out of the grunts—to graduate Marine Corps boot camp as the honor man. This title would mean automatic promotion to Lance

Corporal (E3), skipping two whole pay grades right out of boot camp. Most importantly, it meant selecting the occupation of my choice. This would be my ticket to a Marine Corps experience of my own choosing. Next, I needed to find out how one goes about becoming the honor man. Here is where the story gets interesting.

I would have to be one of two top graduates out of an entire Marine Corps boot camp Company—more than four hundred young men vying for the same honor. A Company is made up of two Series, which is a collection of three separate Platoons. Each Platoon has about seventy recruits. To pull this off, I needed to first become the Guide of my Platoon—the chosen leader of the recruits. I would have to hold on to the position and beat out the Guides from the other two Platoons in the Series to win the title of Series Honor Man. This would be enough to meet the requirements for promotion and my ticket out of the grunts. This victory would place me in the running for the grand prize of Company Honor Man—top graduate out of all 6 platoons. The top dog.

Easy right? Well, not quite but here's the thing—at no point did I ever entertain the thought of not succeeding. How I spent the next four years of my life depended solely on the next 90 days in boot camp. I had my marching orders and I needed to succeed. As Dorothea advised in her book almost eight decades ago, *act as if failure were impossible*. In other words, what if you were so focused on accomplishing a goal that the possibility of failure never entered your mind?

We sat frozen in fear—a crowded bus of terrified and confused teenage boys with badly shaved heads, oversized camouflage uniforms and unpolished combat boots. The Drill Instructor or DI had rushed on the bus and screamed, "Get the f**k off of my bus!" So, we gladly obliged and tripped over ourselves to get the f**k off of his bus.

As we stumbled out onto the pavement, a swarm of angry DIs descended on us from all directions shouting some of the most colorful language I had ever heard in my short 18 years of life. Uncle Sam had just tossed this pack of hungry pit bulls a fresh litter of frightened kittens. These DIs were the epitome of what the Corps refers to as "spit and polished", "squared away", "high and tight". Not a wrinkle in their uniforms or an ounce of fat on their bodies. They were a lot like the guys in the posters, only 100 times scarier. I am sure our predicament caused many of my fellow recruits to question their decision to sign those enlistment papers. Fear and uncertainty held as tight of a grip on me as everyone else, but one particular thought dominated my mind - *I have to be the honor man.*

If you have ever seen Marines marching, the Guide is the guy in front carrying the flag. Gaining this post was the first step. However, something told me not to move too swiftly or to look too eager. I needed to time this perfectly. Little did I realize the time would choose me and not the other way around.

The DIs started by asking for volunteers to be the Guide and the squad leaders. Well, they sort of asked. The request went something like, "Which of you pieces of sh*t thinks he's man enough to lead my platoon!" Several hands shot up because everyone understood the honor and importance of the positions. Only a few of us did not volunteer, myself included. The timing did not feel right.

The next thing I remember is as clear as if it happened yesterday. A young Mexican kid no taller than about 5'5 and slightly overweight rushed to the front to be the Guide, and the DIs promptly planted him at the head of the platoon. His descent from the position would be rapid and frightening.

For the remainder of the day, the DIs berated, humiliated and made a complete fool of this kid. We were all undisciplined, disorganized and looked like total misfits. After all, this was our first day of boot camp. However, our newly appointed Guide was this and much more. The pressure and constant screaming of the DIs proved too much for him as he made mistake after mistake. At times three or four DIs surrounded him and screamed at the top of their lungs. This kid's small frame visibly quivered as these massive mountains of muscle spit out insult after insult. Within a couple of hours they "fired" this poor guy, and sent him to the back of the platoon. I have no recollection of him beyond this point.

Getting fired from a position of honor in boot camp is a regular occurrence, and quite demoralizing. Now the position of Guide was vacant but I still was not ready to make a move. I could not risk getting fired from this position so early in the process. Then, a string of angry words barked through the air that I will never forget - "Jones, get your ass up here! You're my new Guide!"

I had not volunteered but to hesitate for even a fraction of a second would have meant a lost opportunity and even worse verbal abuse. To this day, I have no idea what caused the DI to pick me out of the crowd and at the time I did not care. Success requires speed and I needed to move quickly. So, I double timed to the front of the platoon and took my position. I stood in front feeling totally alone as a fresh pack of DIs surrounded me. Now my turn had come to face humiliation in front of my peers, but all I could think about was one thing - *I have to be the honor man.*

The boot camp experience has this unwritten rule—anyone who becomes the Guide gets fired, often multiple times. I learned this from friends who had entered the Corps ahead of me and came home to tell the rest of us wannabe Leathernecks of their experiences. The issue of getting fired early on was the one that concerned me the most. I would have to chart my course carefully and not stand out too soon.

"Joliet?" One of the DIs said to me as his face contorted in disgust. The wide brim of his smokey sat at an angle almost covering his eyes. The smokey of the Marine Corps Drill Instructor is the most intimidating piece of clothing these guys wear. It is a menacing symbol of power, signifying entrance into a special kind of hell, and the DI with his towering smokey is its gatekeeper.

"The only thing in Joliet is the prison!" He screamed in my face. "Are you from the prison boy?"

"No sir—"

"What the f**k did you say!" another voice came from my left. Something I said infuriated this second DI but I had no idea what. He then moved in closer to me with his smokey almost touching my face. Though I could not look directly at him, I could feel his outrage.

"The first and the last words out that hole in your face is 'Sir.' Do you understand that recruit?"

"Sir, yes sir." I kept my eyes straight ahead conscious not to look directly in the eyes of the DI standing in front of me.

"Joliet, huh?" Apparently, this new DI also had a problem with my hometown. "I bet you was in a gang. That's why you think you're tough—Why you think you can open your hole without saying sir."

"Sir, no sir."
"Don't lie to me recruit. What gang did you belong to?"
"Sir—I, uh—."
"I!" Came yet another voice. All three stood inches from my face cursing and shouting for what most would consider minor infractions. But to these guys, I had broken some serious rules of boot camp etiquette. I just was not sure which rules.

This third DI came from my right. I could only see him from the corner of my eye, but what I saw was enough. "There aint no 'I' here recruit. We don't have individuals in the Corps. But you think you're special 'cause you from Joliet, don't you?"

"Sir—" I wanted so badly to say "I" but caught myself and could not remember which word to use instead.

As if daring me to answer incorrectly, the DI in front lowered his voice to barely a whisper and said, "Sir, what?"

"Sir." Then, I remembered! "Sir, the recruit—." *What was the question!* My mind went blank.

They erupted into a wild symphony of insults and expletives as they closed in even closer. When I think back on it now, I no longer hear words. I see only screaming and furious faces with sprays of spit carry their insults. For what seemed like an eternity, I tripped and stumbled over my words trying to explain I had never been in a gang or in prison—and that I certainly did not think I was special. I did the only thing I could—stood perfectly still with my eyes pointing straight ahead.

"Let's see if you're as dumb as the last one," is the last thing I remember hearing. Somehow, I made it through this onslaught, but this was only the beginning.

Over the next several weeks, there were a number of close calls that almost cost me my position. My biggest challenge was swimming qualification. I never took swimming lessons a day in my life. In fact, I was terrified of the thought drowning, which I am sure was obvious the moment I entered the pool. All that was required was a simple backstroke. For the first few minutes, I thought I would make it until another recruit bumped into me. This broke my concentration and it was as if I had awoke from a dream and found myself in a pool. It did not take long before my arms flailed about as I sucked gulps of water. As my body began to sink, a swim instructor grabbed me and pulled me to the edge of the pool. I hurried out soaked and embarrassed.

"What the f**k Guide, you can't swim?" The instructor shouted these embarrassing words for everyone to hear. "What the hell kind of a Marine can't swim? Get to the other end of the pool with the rest of those clowns."

The dreaded "other end" where all of the non-swimmers are put on display. Here I was the Guide and heading toward the other end of the pool because I could not swim. I would have to go through this entire experience again in third phase, towards the end of boot camp. How I escaped getting fired that day I do not know.

Then, there was the time I had to face my two biggest fears—water and heights. The DIs ordered us to climb a large platform and rope crawl to the other side over a body of water. I remember getting to the top, looking at the rope, then at the water and thinking, *damn*. The distance between platforms looked a mile long and everyone stood below watching and waiting. Turning back and exiting the platform was not an option. Therefore, I took a deep breath, grabbed the rope and headed across, keeping my eyes focused on the sky the entire time. I managed to make it across without making a fool of myself. Exuberance filled every inch of my body as I did my best to mask my excitement.

The day of my imminent dismissal from the position of Guide never came. I made it the entire way through without getting fired. When I tell other Marines this story, they cannot believe it. The day came when I was informed I would go up for Series Honor Man. Once boot camp nears its end, the three Guides from the series compete for this honor by going through an oral interview. A panel of DIs and officers drill the Guides on regulations, Marine Corps history and other items I cannot remember. Then, they eventually get around to asking why you believe you should be the honor man.

As boot camp neared its conclusion, the DIs changed a bit. They did not become friendly necessarily but they began to show some respect and pride for their recruits. It was clearly visible on their faces. They were proud of creating a batch of Marines. By now we were Marines although we still had a few remaining days in boot camp, but this was a mere formality.

When the DI entered the barracks and headed my way, his wide smile was better than words. "Congratulations guide," he said as he held out his hand. "You're the Series Honor Man." *Wow. I did it.*

Now it came down to me and the winning Guide from the competing Series in my Company for the top dog position of Company Honor Man. I would love to report that the fairy tale continued but the other Guide won. According to DIs who explained the outcome to me after boot camp graduation, we scored equally high on the oral interview. This meant the judges had to go to the "paper" to determine the winner—our scores from the rifle range, PFT or physical fitness test and swim qualification. We both scored in the upper ranges for the rifle range and the PFT but his scores were a few points higher in each. Swim qualification—forget it. He qualified as an advanced swimmer, while I qualified two levels lower as a basic swimmer. Despite this, I was still the happiest Marine in San Diego. I met the requirements for promotion and marched across the parade deck in the Marine Corps Dress Blue uniform, an honor reserved for honor graduates. The best part? The occupation of my own choosing. Mission accomplished.

I would later be assigned to the air wing unit at Camp Pendleton, CA called MAG-39. There I made a number of friends whom I still keep contact with to this day. Later I moved to another air wing unit just across the street called HMLA-367. I often volunteered to run paper work over to MAG-39 so I could hang out and joke around with my buddies for a few minutes each day.

One day I went over to drop off some documents and up walks to the counter this little Latin cutie who refused to laugh at any of my jokes. I remember thinking to myself as I left, *what's her problem?—*

In Hindsight

Just as in the story of when I decided to marry my wife, the possibility of failure never crossed my mind—ever. Now this is not to imply that you will be successful one hundred percent of the time by adopting this thinking, but I suspect many of life's challenges would end differently if more people devoted their energy on creative solutions to problems instead all of the reasons why success is implausible.

As I stated from the very beginning, entrepreneurship is about far more than charts and tables—it is about the very heart and soul of those going against odds and so called common sense for something greater and more fulfilling. Even if you fail, at least you took your shot and will never have to ask yourself "what if." I will never have to ask myself: *What if I had picked up the phone and called Escobar? What if I had had the courage to hang in there and ask her to marry me? What if I had had the courage to start my first business? What if only I had the courage to write that book?*

How many "what ifs" have you collected over the years? Decide today once and for all to stop making excuses and take your shot.

Key Take Away

Act as if it were Impossible to Fail!

Recommended Reading in a Nutshell

Never stop learning because life never stops teaching.

Unknown—

As an entrepreneur, especially a beginning entrepreneur, how much time do you have in a given day? Do you have time to read a three hundred page book on entrepreneurship? How about several three hundred page books? I didn't think so, and neither do many of the beginning entrepreneurs I meet. I often find myself sitting with budding entrepreneurs discussing various books on entrepreneurship, selling, business and leadership. I go on to summarize the key points of the books and how to implement the advice. Many times the entrepreneurs apply the information without ever having to read the books.

One of my motivations for writing this book is to combine my experience with what I have learned from some of these books and present it in an easily digestible format. There is a great deal of useful information on the market and I have read a lot of it over the years. So, instead of a simple list of works sited throughout this book, I want to offer a comprehensive list with descriptions of some of my favorites and what I found most useful about them.

But I want to take this a bit further. As someone who is an avid reader to the point of bordering on obsession, I have far more information to share than the short list that follows. I want our relationship to continue. Allow me to do the digging so that you don't have to. As part of my mission to help entrepreneurs increase their odds of succeeding, I am going to distribute, free of charge, a monthly "In a Nutshell" list of books on entrepreneurship for those who subscribe to this book's companion website:

www.PresidentsPilotsEntrepreneurs.com.

The list will detail the key points in the books and how to benefit from the advice. In the meantime, following is a list of books that should be part of every entrepreneur's library. The list is not complete, but represents some of the works I found to be the most useful over the years.

THE 7 HABITS OF HIGHLY EFFECTIVE PEOPLE
STEPHEN R. COVEY

I am always surprised to meet new entrepreneurs who have never heard of this classic. Covey does a fantastic job listing 7 habits, i.e. principles for success in life and in business. One of my favorite habits, "Start with the end in mind," is also a design concept. Instead of focusing on how to do something, focus on what it would look like if it were already done, then start planning from there. This is an absolute must read and is always at the top of my list when talking to new entrepreneurs.

POUR YOUR HEART INTO IT
HOWARD SHULTZ AND DORI JONES YANG

I wish this book was on the market when I first started. This book chronicles the rise of Starbucks from a small coffee bean distributor in Seattle, to the "third place" powerhouse we know it as today. You get the full story right from the mouth of Howard Shultz himself, the CEO of Starbucks and the brainchild of the business. The quote about avoiding banks, which I provided earlier in this book, is by itself worth the price of the book. This book is entrepreneurship in real time.

Customer Centric Selling
Michael T. Bosworth and John R. Holland

Selling is not an art. It is a science according to Bosworth. After reading his book, I must agree. To call something an art is to say one must be an artist. If this is the case for selling, then most of us are in trouble. Bosworth explains in methodical fashion the science of helping the customer buy, instead of attempting to sell them. I internalized much of the advice in this book, and sales meetings turned into conversations about problems and solutions. Honestly, I did not consider it selling as much as diagnosing, which was appreciated by my customers. This is not a quick read, but should be studied by all entrepreneurs and used as a reference. The original edition of this book served as the solution selling bible to many of the world's largest corporations.

Good to Great
Jim Collins

I absolutely fell in love with this book. Jim illustrates that there is no magic or mystery behind successful companies, but a deliberate process that they all have in common. This can be duplicated by any company, whether large or small. Jim says there are three interconnected circles to focus your attention: that which you do better than anyone else, understanding your economic engine (the driver of your revenues), and that which you are most passionate about. Combine these three and you create something that no one can compete against. Jim also proves this is why companies in the same industry, economy and geographic location get opposite results. It is because of the intersection between these three interconnected circles, which he refers to as the hedgehog concept. This one is an easy read. Get it.

THE LAWS OF SUCCESS
NAPOLEON HILL

This is more of a course than a book. Napoleon Hill is also the author of "Think and Grow Rich", which you may have already heard of. The Laws of Success, a sixteen volume college style course, is "Think and Grow Rich" on steroids. This is a set of lessons in sound, universal principles of success and is the basis for many of today's books on leadership, entrepreneurship and self help. It is a lengthy series and must be studied, not simply read. Far from just thinking positive, Hill explains the specific actions required that go along with right thinking in order to achieve success. This classic is available for download from many legitimate sources all over the Internet. Read this series even if it takes you months to complete.

THINK AND GROW RICH
NAPOLEON HILL

This is a primer to "The Laws of Success" and also a must read. I read this book before reading its larger cousin and found it more beneficial than I can describe in a few sentences. This book is a great place to start before diving into The Laws of Success. Hill not only has amazing anecdotes but is also a great story teller. The way he explains his personal trials and triumphs is enough to inspire even the most pessimistic among us.

WAKE UP AND LIVE!
DOROTHEA BRANDE

Dorothea Brande wrote this fantastic little book in 1936. Besides her philosophy on acting as if failure were impossible, Dorothea gives a detailed explanation of what she refers to as "the will to fail." She discusses how people consciously and unconsciously set themselves up to fail to avoid taking responsibility for the results. This book is a fascinating read. Books like Dorothea's make me wonder why so many authors insist on books of three hundred pages or more when they could pack an even heavier punch with half the words. Dorothea's book is an example of crisp, to the point and impactful writing

EXECUTION
LARRY BOSSIDY AND RAM CHARAN

The title of the book says it all. The focus is on seeing ideas and plans through to proper execution—the "how." The book identifies three core processes of proper execution: people, strategy and operations. This book is to be studied carefully and used as a reference, not read casually while watching the news. Add it to your library to understand how to properly operate your business.

THE ALCHEMIST
PAOLO COELHO

Some may wonder why I include a short book of fiction in this section. Well, teachers are all around for those with wide open eyes and minds. Paolo's book is about having the courage to follow the path towards your goals regardless of where it takes you. There are times we will not understand the things that happen along the way, but if we have the faith and conviction to follow our hearts, we will eventually find our success. Be forewarned, however, as success may not look quite the way we expected. This is another easy read and yet another example of why shorter books pack more of a punch.

Well, there you have my short list, which includes the books I mentioned throughout this work as well as a couple of others. I wish there was more space to go into the details of these books, but I promised to keep this work short. However, there is no space limit on the Internet so be sure to subscribe to my blog at:

www.PresidentsPilotsEntrepreneurs.com

to get my monthly "In a Nutshell" summary of some of the most useful entrepreneurship and leadership books both past and present. As for the books in the above list, I recommend of full read at some point. Otherwise, you can get the Key Takeaways "In a Nutshell" from the blog.

JOIN THE REVOLUTION!

It is literally true that you can succeed best and quickest by helping others succeed.
Napoleon Hill—

Join Derrick on the web:
www.PresidentsPilotsEntrepreneurs.com
for more insights and advice for beginning entrepreneurs.

Or on Facebook:
www.Facebook.com/PPEBOOK

Twitter Handle:
@djoneslucid

Subscribe to Derrick's blog to gain access to the new "In a Nutshell" newsletter where Derrick summarizes the Key Take Aways from some the most popular books on entrepreneurship, business, sales and leadership. You may even be featured in Derrick's upcoming book where he reserves a special section for some of the most compelling entrepreneur survival stories.

Join the revolution today and help increase the success rate of entrepreneurs!

About the Author

Derrick Jones is a serial entrepreneur with three tech startups under his belt. He resides in upstate New York with his wife Lisa of twenty years and their five children. Derrick is a frequent speaker at colleges and trade organizations on the subjects of entrepreneurship and leadership. He is also a regular speaker at high schools where he encourages students to use technology for more than taking in information but to also share their talents with the world.

Made in the USA
Charleston, SC
23 December 2012